"*Mending the Heart* is an excellent reso through step-by-step encouragement wh nuts and bolts of the annulment process. shows how to look beyond civil court rul from the 'cross of divorce' to become a better, wiser, and stronger person, and to experience happiness and peace again. The author's compassionate and practical voice as someone who has keenly experienced the pain of divorce and has been healed through the transforming annulment process is sure to strike a chord with every reader. I highly recommend this book."

— DONNA-MARIE COOPER O'BOYLE, EWTN-TV host, pilgrimage host, speaker, and award-winning and best-selling author of more than twenty-five books, including her memoir, *The Kiss of Jesus: How Mother Teresa and the Saints Helped Me to Discover the Beauty of the Cross* (www.donnacooperoboyle.com)

———

"Lisa Duffy gently holds your hand and accompanies you in the difficult journey of divorce in *Mending the Heart: A Catholic Annulment Companion.* Lisa concisely and compassionately explains common myths and misconceptions, often perpetuated by secular media, about the annulment process. She explains what the Catholic Church really teaches about marriage, divorce, and annulments. This book is a must read for anyone going through this process!"

— MARY LOU ROSIEN, author of *The Three Things Divorced Catholics Need to Know* and blogger at Catholicmom.com

"Lisa Duffy offers a compassionate, practical, and deeply personal exploration of the annulment process that proves how truly healing the process can be."

— LORENE HANLEY DUQUIN, author of *Seeking an Annulment with the Help of Your Catholic Faith*

———

"Lisa Duffy takes the stressful and sometimes painful process of applying for a declaration of invalidity and makes it easier for the mind — and the heart — to digest. She opens a window to the process and lets in the light of truth and grace. As a canon lawyer, I found it refreshing to read a heartfelt book that covers the truth of the process and gives people hope. Anyone who feels overwhelmed emotionally by the invalidity process should read this book and take heed of its guidance."

— JACQUI RAPP, JD, JCL, MCL (kycanonist.com), author of *Annulment: 100 Questions and Answers for Catholics*

Mending the Heart

A Catholic Annulment Companion

LISA DUFFY

mending
the
HEART

A CATHOLIC
ANNULMENT COMPANION

**Our
Sunday
Visitor**

www.osv.com
Our Sunday Visitor Publishing Division
Our Sunday Visitor, Inc.
Huntington, Indiana 46750

Nihil Obstat
Msgr. Michael Heintz, Ph.D.
Censor Librorum

Imprimatur
✠ Kevin C. Rhoades
Bishop of Fort Wayne-South Bend
November 11, 2017

The *Nihil Obstat* and *Imprimatur* are official declarations that a book is free from doctrinal or moral error. It is not implied that those who have granted the *Nihil Obstat* and *Imprimatur* agree with the contents, opinions, or statements expressed.

Our Sunday Visitor Publishing Division, Our Sunday Visitor, Inc., 200 Noll Plaza, Huntington, IN 46750; 1-800-348-2440

ISBN: 978-1-68192-149-5 (Inventory No. T1869)
eISBN: 978-1-68192-151-8
LCCN: 2017958842

Cover design: Chelsea Alt
Cover art: Shutterstock
Interior design: Lindsey Riesen
Interior art: Photos on page 111 courtesy of the contributors.

PRINTED IN THE UNITED STATES OF AMERICA

ABOUT THE AUTHOR

LISA DUFFY is a Catholic author, speaker, and divorce recovery expert who experienced the tragedy of an unwanted divorce in the early 1990s. She has nearly twenty years of personal experience helping people rebuild their lives after divorce. Author of many books on divorce recovery and a personal divorce recovery coach, she has also instituted the Journey of Hope program for Catholic divorce support groups in parishes across the United States and in Canada. Aside from her dedication to her family, Lisa speaks at conferences, appears on television and radio, coaches one-on-one and in groups, and holds online events. She resides in South Carolina with her husband and three children.

For all those who have suffered through the devastation of divorce,

For all the priests, canon lawyers, and parish case assistants who read our painful stories and accompany us through the process with patience and compassion,

For all the lay people who generously donate their time and care as divorce support group leaders, I dedicate this book to you.

———

But mostly, for Jim, who has always been an endless source of wisdom, encouragement, consolation, and support. Thank you for being the best husband in the world.

TABLE OF CONTENTS

INTRODUCTION

Imagine for a moment sitting in your car in the parking lot of a busy Denny's restaurant around five o'clock in the afternoon. You haven't slept or eaten much in the last two weeks. You're dealing with dehydration because you've cried every tear your body could possibly produce, yet somehow you could still cry a river at the drop of a hat.

This was me back in August 1993. I was sitting in my car, mustering up the courage to go inside that restaurant and meet with my soon-to-be ex-husband. Two weeks before this day, he had walked out and filed for divorce. He had lived a double life for our entire marriage. I had also lost three children in miscarriage by this point, and after surgery to correct the problem I was told by doctors I was sterile. I now had a less than 1 percent chance of ever conceiving a child. The pain I felt was so heavy in my heart, it felt as if it would physically crush me.

The priest who had been counseling me during those two weeks had been very compassionate, but he also told me I had to ask my husband to consider reconciliation. At first, I was insulted and offended at the suggestion. After all, I was not the one who had left! I was not the one who had been unfaithful! What in the world would possess me to put myself in such a vulnerable position? How humiliating! But the more I thought about it, the more I knew Father Joe was right. I knew that if I didn't at least throw the offer of reconciliation out there, I would always look back and wonder, "What if?" What if I could have done more to save my marriage?

My heart was pounding so hard I thought I would have a heart attack. My hands were shaking, and I didn't know if I would be able to talk, but I had convinced myself that I had to do this. So I

13

went inside and sat down at the table and waited for him. When he arrived, I could see he had visibly changed. The man I married was gone, and now someone very cold and indifferent was in his place. That was probably the most painful conversation I have ever had, and I will never forget it. My request was declined. There was no going back. Soon, regardless of the fact that I took my vows seriously and had married for life, the no-fault divorce laws would ensure that I would be divorced.

The next few years for me were like wandering in the desert, never finding an oasis. I made a lot of mistakes during that period of my life, choices that only brought more pain. I blamed my ex-spouse for everything, even two years later, which made me a victim. And the sad truth is, victims never heal. They just stay stuck in their misery.

And then came an epiphany of sorts — I realized I was just sick and tired of being sick and tired all the time. I didn't like this version of myself. I didn't like being a victim. So I decided I would change. Part of that change was starting the annulment process. I had heard conflicting reports from various people about the annulment process — personal horror stories or warnings, mostly — but I felt compelled to give it a chance. I needed to restart my life, and if that were to happen I had to face the truth of my past.

I eventually received a decree of invalidity in 1997, and in June 2000 I got married in the Church to my husband, Jim. And despite what the doctors said, we have three beautiful, healthy teenagers. God has blessed me immensely!

I share that with you because you are likely reading this book because you or someone you know has gone through a divorce, and you are looking for answers about the Catholic annulment process. But, if I may guess, you don't just want technical answers about the process. You want to know what the experience is like, yes? You're seeking answers to deeper questions as I was. Questions like: How in the world did I end up here? How could God allow my marriage to end in divorce? Am I still accepted in my Church? And probably most importantly: Where do I go from here?

These are critical questions that deserve answers, and I've written this book in the hope of helping you find those answers.

Some answers you will find in the black and white on these pages, and some you will find through self-reflection and prayer. As you read this book, the information will naturally cause you to pause, remember, and reflect on some pretty deep things. I always find that when this part of the healing process takes place, it is most helpful to unite those remembrances and reflections in conversation with God because he will illuminate your thought process and speak to your heart.

In the Old Testament book of Ecclesiastes, we read a very bittersweet passage:

> For everything there is a season, and a time
> for every matter under heaven:
> a time to be born, and a time to die;
> a time to plant, and a time to pluck up what is planted;
> a time to kill, and a time to heal;
> a time to break down, and a time to build up;
> a time to weep, and a time to laugh;
> a time to mourn, and a time to dance;
> a time to cast away stones, and a time to gather stones together;
> a time to embrace, and a time to refrain from embracing;
> a time to seek, and a time to lose;
> a time to keep, and a time to cast away;
> a time to tear, and a time to sew;
> a time to keep silence, and a time to speak;
> a time to love, and a time to hate;
> a time for war, and a time for peace. (Eccles 3:1–8)

This passage is bittersweet because at least half of it seems to negate our reasons for living. "A time to kill ... a time for war ... a time to tear down ... a time to mourn" — these words directly contradict the sense of hope for the future that has been instilled in us since childhood. Life should be happy, and the promise of future happiness should never pale. But it does. Our lives are filled with crosses, big and small. The cross of divorce, in my opinion, is one of the heaviest you can bear. So I offer you these words of wisdom from Scripture, not to emphasize the tragedies that befall us, but to underscore the truth that with every suffering we encounter comes growth and refreshment. With every challenge, there can be triumph, for Ecclesiastes also promises "a time to heal ... a time to laugh ... a time to dance."

And that is what God intends for you despite your divorce: personal triumph.

It begins with simply understanding that nothing you could ever do can make God love you less. It doesn't matter if you initiated your divorce or if your ex-spouse did. God loves you as much today as the day he breathed life into your soul in your mother's womb. Despite all the heartbreak of losing your marriage, God wants to heal you.

I speak from experience. I never wanted to be divorced, but it happened anyway. The pain I endured for so many years felt as though it should have killed me, and at times I thought it would. But it didn't. And the very fact that it didn't speaks of the great hope there is for each of us. If the pain and suffering is so terrible that it feels as though you'll die, but you continue to live, it means there is hope, there is a future, and God still has good things in store for you.

But how do you go from being desperately miserable to happy again? One very important step you can take is the Catholic annulment process. In my experience, although it was difficult to sift through the details of my failed marriage and revisit painful memories, it changed me. It helped me become a better, wiser, stronger person. It helped me accept the truth of what had happened and recognize that, although I fought for my marriage, I had contributed to the divorce. I had not been a perfect spouse. This was very freeing for me. And in the end, it helped me come to terms with the fact that we never had a valid marriage in the eyes of God. That's what the annulment process does: it brings clarity on all fronts. These are the reasons why I encourage you to consider going through this healing process yourself.

Not every divorced Catholic is *required* to go through the annulment process — only those who want to remarry in the Church. If you don't see yourself ever marrying again, you are not compelled to apply for the annulment process. Yet you still might consider doing it for a few important reasons. First, going through the annulment process offers a level of healing that is unique and difficult to find through any other means. Also, the annulment process offers you the opportunity to know without a doubt where you stand with the Church after your divorce. Everyone deserves the chance to have this confirmation and clarity. There are spiritual and eternal ramifications to divorce and annulment. That is precisely why the Catholic Church offers the annulment process, so that you can look beyond what a civil court has ruled and the social implications of divorce to what the actual spiritual reality may be.

Just thinking about starting the Catholic annulment process can be very confusing. There is a lot of material out there, and much of it is unhelpful. Myths and misinformation have been perpetuated for many years, and too many people — both within the Church and outside — have accepted them as truth. Following Pope Francis' changes to the annulment process in 2015, and the inaccurate reporting from the secular media about what those changes entailed, things have gotten even more puzzling, and it can be tough to know where to look for answers.

Rest assured, you are not alone in seeking answers. There are millions of Catholics, both divorced and non-divorced, who do not understand what the annulment process is all about. And because this is truly a legal process within the Church, the language is not necessarily easy to grasp. As a result, people don't feel comfortable looking to the primary sources for information, and they fall prey to the wide range of myths and misinformation that others, who also do not understand, have circulated.

It is my hope that in reading this book, you will not only receive the answers you are seeking but also a greater sense of the hope and healing that can come from going through the annulment process.

CHAPTER ONE

"A Time to Tear, and a Time to Sew"

What the Annulment Process Really Is and Why It Matters

It happened on a Sunday afternoon.

I was walking my dog at the local park that sunny summer day in 1993, trying to think positive thoughts — but my heart was filled with dread, and I knew something bad was coming. As I made my way back to the house, I saw my husband's black Toyota Celica come racing down the street. I went inside and waited for him. He had been gone for several days without a phone call or an explanation, and as he walked into the kitchen, he announced he was leaving me and filing for divorce.

My life was completely torn apart. I pleaded with him to reconsider his decision, to at least explain why he was leaving, but the most I could get out of him was that we had grown apart, and that now he wanted different things out of life than he had when we got married.

Of course, I was devastated. I did not want to get divorced, and I was willing to do whatever it took to make the marriage work. Not only had I married for life, but I was Catholic, and I knew that Catholics are not supposed to get divorced. This is because the Catholic Church upholds Christ's teaching that marriage was created to be a permanent union — so really, no one is supposed to get divorced, but Catholics are bound by that teaching.

But my husband would not change his mind. My life changed dramatically from that day forward. The life I had worked so hard to build during the years we were married began being dismantled piece by piece as we went through the legal process of separation and divorce. I would now have to figure out what kind of future was in store for me. I would need to figure out how to put the pieces back together, how to mend my life.

Finding My Way Back to the Future

Like anyone who gets divorced, I had to find a way to start again and forge a new future for myself. The hard part was knowing where to begin. Of course, I had a lot of questions, many of them about how I would reconcile the fact that I was now both divorced and Catholic: Could I still receive the sacraments? Was I still welcome at church? Was God ashamed of me?

Little by little, I received answers from the priest who was counseling me during that time. And after getting myself through those first horrible months of overwhelming pain — pain so intense that it felt as though I should have died because of it, I began to wonder about the annulment process and whether or not it was right for me. I was thirty years old at the time, and although my preference was to reconcile with my husband and remain married, that option had been declined by my ex-spouse. Looking ahead to the future, the idea of being alone for the rest of my life seemed like cruel and unusual punishment. I was confident my vocation in life was to marriage, and I was distraught at the idea of facing the future by myself.

I really didn't know anything about the annulment process, just that it was an option for Catholics in my position. Yet every time I entertained the idea of "getting an annulment" — as I had heard it put so many times — I had this nagging feeling that something wasn't quite right.

How could it be that I stood before God, family, and friends the day we got married and pledged my life to my husband, for better or for worse, but suddenly the State of California could step in and declare my marriage was over? It was supposed to be a permanent relationship. How does that happen? Before the ink had barely dried on the divorce papers, my ex-spouse was calling someone else his wife. According to just about everyone else, that was it. Our marriage was over. But I was convinced there had to be more to it than that. It seemed so easy — *too* easy — for something that was supposed to last forever to be suddenly over at the crack of a gavel. Something was very wrong and unsettling about that.

There was a lot I needed to do before I could consider the possibility of going through the annulment process. I had so many questions, and it was a bit overwhelming. Many people I talked to about it had varying opinions — sometimes polar opposites — and I ended up not really knowing what to think.

Your circumstances may be altogether different from mine. Maybe you were not abandoned by your spouse but were pushed to the point of making the choice to divorce because of some sort of abuse. There are many scenarios that could bring you to this point. But no matter what your situation is, you probably also feel that there has to be more to the annulment process than receiving a simple, albeit expensive, piece of paper. I'd like to walk down this path with you and help you sort through this complex situation. If there is a time to tear, and in this sense I refer to the shredding of a marriage contract, then there definitely is a time to mend, a time to heal. And from my perspective, the annulment process truly is a time for mending and healing.

My goal in this chapter is to start with the basic premise of the annulment process and discuss in simple terms what it actually is, and why it can be important to go through it.

Our Unfortunate Reality

God designed marriage to be a permanent, exclusive, lifelong relationship that is open to new life. Strong marriages and families are the building blocks of society. Our unfortunate reality, however, is that divorce has become commonplace, even expected, and many Catholics today find themselves divorced, whether intentionally or not. For some, divorce is an excuse to exit an unhappy marriage. For others, it is forced upon them, whether they are the abandoned spouse or are compelled to choose that option as a means of protection from an abusive relationship. This is not some bogus way of saying divorce is okay, because it's *not* okay. But it is the reality we live in, and it is a crisis we need to deal with on a realistic level.

So the Catholic Church offers us an effective tool for clarification and healing in the annulment process. You might think of it as the Church's way of helping people set the record straight and move forward in life with certainty when a state's government has ruled that a marriage contract ceases to exist. Because we, as Catholics, don't believe marriage is just a simple legal contract but an actual institution and sacrament, there are far more ramifications than just dividing property and parting ways.

The annulment process can seem intimidating and over-whelming if you are standing on the outside looking in. Many people who consider starting this process wonder whether or not it is worthwhile to spend their time and energy rehashing the past and all its painful memories. This aspect of the process is deeply sobering and can be quite intimidating. The whole thing can also sound like a lot of legal hassle — filling out forms and selecting witnesses for testimony, in-person depositions with canon lawyers, etc. If you've just gone through a court battle for a civil divorce, going through yet another legal procedure for the Church probably doesn't seem very palatable.

A good friend of mine, Dan Flaherty, shares his perspective:

My view of the annulment process going in was that it was just "Catholic divorce" — not so much in theory, where I understood the teaching of the Church, but in terms of the way it was actually practiced. I believed that the tribunals simply processed the applications like bureaucrats.

My one-on-one interview with a tribunal representative was different. The person questioning me was compassionate and non-judgmental, yet still looking for information. In contrast to the divorce courts, which only asked how assets were to be divided, the tribunal rep was asking questions about conditions prior to the marriage, in terms of both the relationship and with me as an individual.

I still recall at one point recounting something in particular and shuddering. A nerve was hit. Deep down, I knew that the marriage had been doomed from the start, and everything about the process — from the personal interview to the questionnaire — confirmed me in that belief.

One thing I would also say to anyone entering the annulment process is that you get out of it what you put into it. I chose to treat it as a time when I was in a spiritual hospital, as it were. I began seeing a Catholic therapist. It's certainly possible to go through the process and get only minimal benefit — the number of times I actually spoke to the tribunal or wrote a document couldn't have been more than two–three times over the course of a year-plus. But if you take the wounds that are exposed during those handfuls of times and work on them outside the annulment process, you get the most this healing time can offer.

I can't say the sense of guilt over the failure of the marriage has gone away, but today it is manageable. It wasn't when I began the process.

You might read Dan's story and know exactly what he is describing. Stories like his are common among people entertaining the idea of going through the annulment process.

So let's unpack all of this and try to get to a basic understanding of it.

A Simple Breakdown of the Annulment Process

Simply put, the annulment process is a tool. Using the details you provide about your marriage relationship, the people involved in the annulment process — you, your ex-spouse, the case assistant (someone appointed by a parish to help walk you through the process), and the canon lawyers — can create a "big picture" scenario to determine whether or not a valid marriage was brought into being on the day of your wedding. Just as a doctor uses tools to detect what might be ailing you — a stethoscope, an X-ray machine, an electrocardiogram — the information you provide and the testimony of your witnesses are tools that assist the tribunal in being able to see what caused your marriage to fail. More importantly, this information helps them determine whether or not you had a valid marriage bond to begin with. This brings us to a very important theme that goes along with the impact of the annulment process: whether or not you had a *valid marriage.*

For my part, this assertion that I may not have had a valid marriage was one of the most difficult aspects I wrestled with when I was contemplating whether or not to go through the annulment process. The mere idea sounded insulting because I knew without a doubt that I had taken my vows seriously, and to consider the possibility that the marriage never was valid to begin with felt like a hit below the belt. But once I understood what it all really meant, it actually brought a lot of clarity to the whole idea of taking this step.

What Is a Valid Marriage Bond?

People have different ideas about what marriage really is. Some people believe that every marriage is permanent and unbreakable, no matter who you are or under what circumstances you were married. From this perspective, it doesn't matter if you were married in a church with a full Catholic Mass, on a beach with the local Unitarian minister presiding, or at a Vegas wedding chapel with Elvis as your witness. In each of these scenarios, so goes the logic, the couple took vows, so the marriage must be valid.

On the other extreme, many people today believe a marriage is only permanent when both spouses mutually agree that it should be. From this perspective, regardless of *how* the marriage happened, if there comes a time where one or both spouses decide their relationship is not working, they can determine that their marriage is no longer valid. If they make that decision, then they are no longer bound to each other and can go their separate ways.

Both of these perspectives are wrong.

The truth is that some marriages are valid and some marriages are not. It has absolutely nothing to do with personal opinion. It has everything to do with *understanding* and *intention* upon entering the marriage. A valid marriage is a permanent and unbreakable bond in the eyes of God, and not every couple who says "I do" brings this valid bond into being. The difference has to do with what takes place on the day of the wedding and leading up to that point. It has little to do with what happens after the wedding day.

If a couple wishes to bring a valid marriage into being on their wedding day, the following things must take place:

- Both spouses must come to the wedding of their own free will.
- Both spouses must intend to make a lifelong, exclusive commitment to each other.
- Both spouses must be open to new life and bringing children into the world.
- A Catholic priest or deacon must be present at the wedding.

In other words, to bring a valid marriage into being, the couple needs to know what marriage is about, and they need to enter into it freely, with full intention. The first three of the points above are rooted in the "unitive" and "procreative" aspects of marriage — what the Catholic Church has defined as the two basic reasons for marriage: to unite the husband and wife to each other in love and to prepare a welcoming home for any children God may send. When these elements are present, a valid marriage bond is created.

Valid vs. Sacramental
Let's clarify a few terms here that might be confusing. For the purposes of the annulment process, the terms "valid" and "sacramental" are apples and oranges. "Valid" refers to the fact that the couple stood in the right place, said the right things, and intended the right things. "Sacramental" refers to a valid marriage that has been contracted by spouses who are both baptized Christians.[1] So, a Catholic and a Catholic can have a sacramental marriage, as can a Baptist and a Lutheran, or a Catholic and an Episcopalian, etc. But, for a marriage to be sacramental, both spouses must be baptized. So a Catholic and a Hindu cannot create a sacramental marriage, nor a Lutheran and a Jew. Marriages that are not between two baptized Christians are referred to as "natural"

---

1. "From a valid marriage arises *a bond* between the spouses which by its very nature is perpetual and exclusive; furthermore, in a Christian marriage the spouses are strengthened and, as it were, consecrated for the duties and the dignity of their state *by a special sacrament*" (*Catechism of the Catholic Church* [CCC], 1638, emphasis in original).

marriages, meaning a marriage that is permanent, exclusive, open to children, and ordered to the good of the spouses, but one or both spouses are not baptized Christians.

In the annulment process, the canon lawyers are trying to determine whether a marriage — regardless of its sacramental or non-sacramental nature — is actually valid or invalid.

Our Goal as Catholics

For a Catholic getting married to another baptized person, the goal is to bring a valid, sacramental marriage into being on the day of the wedding. (A Catholic who marries someone who is not baptized must first obtain a dispensation from the local bishop. If the marriage is permitted, a sacramental marriage is not possible, but a valid marriage definitely is possible.) This sacramental bond is an unbreakable covenant between God and the spouses, and the only thing that can dissolve it is death.

Pope Francis describes this perfectly in his 2016 apostolic exhortation, *Amoris Laetitia* ("The Joy of Love"):

> The sacrament of marriage is not a social convention, an empty ritual or merely the outward sign of a commitment. The sacrament is a gift given for the sanctification and salvation of the spouses, since "their mutual belonging is a real representation, through the sacramental sign, of the same relationship between Christ and the Church...."
>
> "In accepting each other, and with Christ's grace, the engaged couple promise each other total self-giving, faithfulness and openness to new life. The couple recognizes these elements as constitutive of marriage, gifts offered to them by God, and take seriously their mutual commitment, in God's name and in the presence of the Church." (72–73)

To Dissolve or Not to Dissolve

Some years back, I was talking to a divorced woman, Sandy, who was feeling discouraged about her future after going through a divorce. She believed that now, because she was Catholic, she was just stuck being single for the rest of her life, and she was only thirty-nine. I asked her if she had been through the annulment process to see if she actually could remarry at some point, and she quickly replied, "Oh, I don't believe in the annulment process. I don't believe the Church can take away the vows I took."

Sandy is not alone in her *mis*interpretation of what the annulment process actually accomplishes. A common assumption is that the annulment process is simply a legal process to go through, a sort of "Catholic divorce." Often, this confusion comes from the language used regarding the process. People say things like, "You need to get an annulment," which makes it sound as if anyone can go down to some office, fill out a few papers, and receive some kind of legal document that declares the former marriage null and permits the divorcee to marry again. If you have a sense of what marriage ought to be, this should give you an uneasy feeling.

Because marriage is supposed to be much more than an empty ritual or just an outward sign of commitment, the annulment process is also much more than an administrative process. It is a vehicle to help bring the wounded from the battlefield into the field hospital, where they can find healing, if I may paraphrase Pope Francis.

Rest assured, receiving a decree of invalidity does not mean your marriage *relationship* never existed. This is a painful misconception that holds many people back from starting the annulment process. After putting in all that hard work, no one wants to be told their relationship was somehow not real. Nor is the annulment process just a sneaky way for the Church to allow spouses to get out of a bad marriage. The Church is not looking for a loophole or for some way to declare a marriage that is permanent in the eyes of God to be no longer valid.

Perhaps the worst thing about these misconceptions is that they completely ignore the greater aspect of the annulment process: the opportunity to face the truth about what happened, make peace with the past and lay it to rest, and find spiritual and emotional healing from divorce.

So the natural questions that arise are: If the purpose of the annulment process isn't to dissolve a valid marriage bond, and it's not some loophole in the moral law, then how can people get remarried after a divorce? Why must you go through the annulment process after a civil divorce has been obtained?

Will the Real Annulment Process Please Stand Up?

The real purpose of the Catholic annulment process is to determine whether or not a valid marriage bond was brought into being on the day of your wedding. As we discussed before, not all marriages have a valid bond. Some marriages have the *appearance* of being valid but do not have a valid bond. We know that a valid marriage is one that takes place between a man and a woman who come to the altar with the desire to create a permanent union with an openness to having children. (Note: This would include couples who are unable to have children but still marry with the desire to create a lifelong, permanent relationship and an openness to new life if God chooses to bless them with that gift. A couple can still have a valid marriage even if they are not able to have children.) As previously mentioned, the Catholic Church teaches that marriage is a sacrament. So, in addition to the unitive and procreative aspects needed to form a valid union, it takes two baptized Christians to form a sacramental marriage.

But some marriages only appear to be valid when they actually are not. How does that happen? Well, think of it this way. For a sacrament to take place, two things *must* be present: matter and form. To understand what these two elements are, take a look at the Mass. A priest can pray the words of Eucharistic consecration (the form) over an Oreo cookie, but it cannot be changed into the Body of Christ because that is not the proper matter. The host must be unleavened wheat bread. Likewise, even if the proper host is on the altar, I cannot pray the words of consecration over it: only an ordained Catholic priest can. To take another example, look at Baptism. If you try to baptize someone with Coca-Cola, there is no valid baptism. You must use water (matter) and say the appropriate blessing (form) during the pouring of the water.

The same is true for a marriage. All the right things must be in place for a marriage to be valid. The form of the Sacrament of Matrimony is the vows themselves, while the matter is the couple's mutual consent and the consummation of the marriage. Often, it appears that a couple has everything they need for a valid marriage — they can check off the usual boxes, the service at the church, the dress, tux, rings, certificate, etc. But if the two people exchanging their vows do not fully intend the unitive and procreative aspects of marriage, a valid bond cannot be created.

In my own experience, anyone who attended my wedding back in 1990 probably would not have questioned the validity of our marriage based upon what they saw. He and I were both Catholic, and we got married in a beautiful Catholic church with a full Mass. We had the dress, the tux, the rings, a handsome bridal party, and flowers. We had all the right things in all the right places except for the most critical aspect: intentions. My then-spouse later admitted *many* disturbing things about that day and the days leading up to the wedding. The most unfortunate thing, in my opinion, was that he never had any intention of remaining faithful or remaining married. He knew going into it that at some point he would leave. This is an example of how a couple can appear to have a valid marriage when they really don't.

Permanent Ain't So Permanent After All

Situations such as mine are more and more common these days, especially caused by the attitudes and perspectives of society. Many generations of divorce have diluted the notion that marriage is permanent, and the rise in cohabitation contributes to the idea that family relationships are interchangeable. There are untold numbers of couples getting married today who do not have any understanding of what marriage is supposed to be.

Terry describes what it was like to come to this realization as he went through the annulment process. He was married to his wife, Allison, for about six years before he filed for divorce, and he shares part of his experience:

I never dreamed I would ever do such a thing. When we got married, I thought the rest of our lives would be great, but Allison's constant, unrepentant infidelity made me realize I had no other option. Our five-year-old son was being neglected and negatively affected by seeing his mother with other men. I couldn't just stand by and do nothing. Now he and I are just trying to live as normal lives as possible.

Reading through the annulment questionnaire was difficult at first, but ultimately, it opened my eyes to what had really happened. I recognized things I couldn't see when Allison and I were first dating and in love. Growing up, Allison's family had many struggles with abuse, which she rarely talked about because it upset her. After discussing it once with me, she would change the subject whenever I brought up the issue. It never occurred to me that this was something that could pose a problem; I just thought she wanted me to respect her privacy.

I was always amazed that Allison said yes when I asked her to marry me because she was such a popular girl. We got married shortly after college, but in hindsight, I don't think she ever was really interested in being a mom or a wife; she just wanted a different life than what she had. When she got tired of me, she ran to someone else for gratification. This was the hard truth I had to come to terms with.

Subconsciously, I know I was not willing to admit this before, but in having to write it all down, it really helped me to accept this about us and find peace. I felt like I could begin to move forward.

Terry's case is not that unusual, and it illustrates how a couple can have the appearance of a valid marriage on the outside but not truly have one. Allison did not come to the altar with the intention of marrying for life. She also had emotional issues that, left unaddressed, became an obstacle to her being able to fully commit herself as a spouse. This brings us to the next, natural question: What kinds of situations would make a couple incapable of having a valid marriage?

The Obstacles

Situations that can prevent a couple from bringing a valid marriage into being on the day of their wedding are called "obstacles," and they can arise in many different areas:

- First, the bride and the groom must have complete freedom to give themselves to each other. When might this not be the case? There could be pressure from parents to get married, or maybe the bride is pregnant. Maybe the marriage is taking place only to secure citizenship in a particular country. These are examples of circumstances that would constitute a deficiency and would prohibit the bride and groom from creating a valid bond.
- Moreover, the bride and the groom must come to the altar with the intention of creating a lifelong marriage relationship and accepting children as God gives them (the unitive and procreative aspects of marriage). If either of these intentions is absent from the bride's or the groom's perspective, a valid marriage cannot take place.
- Next, both the bride and the groom must have complete understanding of the vows they are taking, and they need to possess the emotional and psychological ability to live them.
- Finally, the marriage must be consummated. If a couple has the wedding, but they never consummate the marriage, their union is not indissoluble. This is a special case, and such marriages would require a special dispensation from the pope to be dissolved.

Going through the annulment process and finding that an impediment existed to making a valid bond between you and your former spouse can be very difficult. This is especially hard to accept if you stood at the altar with full freedom and love, with full understanding and the proper intentions, but you come to realize that your ex-spouse may not have had the same intentions, understanding, or freedom. And it may also be that something about your intention or understanding was where the impediment lay. In chapter 4, author and annulment consultant Rose Sweet will offer an example of this for us in the story she shares.

Don't despair. With God's grace, coming to recognize the truth about your relationship can have a cleansing effect that will help

you deal with the breakdown of your marriage as you go through
this process.

A Little Encouragement

Hopefully, the information you've read so far has brought things
a little more into focus and given you a firmer grasp on what
the Catholic annulment process is all about. You may still be
apprehensive about proceeding, however, because it may still seem
too technical, legalistic, or even painful for you, and that's okay.
What you've been through is devastating, and it should not be taken
lightly. I encourage you to take your time. But I want to assure you
that, if you can enter into it with a sincere desire to understand the
past and discover what new path God may have for you, you will
find the annulment process to be very healing. There is a cleansing
of emotional wounds that takes place and an authentic sense of
closure that allows you to move forward and rebuild your life.

The annulment process provides a level of healing from the loss
of a marriage that is unique because of its thorough, spiritual nature.
You won't find this anywhere else. It also offers you the opportunity
to look back at your marriage relationship and understand how
and why it failed. At the same time, the process helps you to accept
the role you played in the divorce and stop blaming your ex-spouse.
Finally, the process gives you the opportunity to learn from what
happened and make better choices in the future.

The best way to approach the annulment process is with the
attitude of discerning God's will for your life after your divorce.
No matter what the decision, you will come away from this process
with a definitive direction. You will have clarity and confidence in
where to go from that point forward, whether it be marriage or the
single life. Be assured, no matter what happens, God still has a plan
for you, and the annulment process frees you to live it out.

QUICK POINTS RECAP

- The annulment process does not dissolve a valid marriage bond; it simply detects whether or not there was one to begin with.

- To bring a valid marriage into being, a couple must have:

  > Complete freedom to give themselves to each other.

  > Proper understanding and intention to create a permanent, exclusive relationship that is open to life (unitive and procreative aspects).

  > A priest or deacon as a witness.

  > Consummation.

- A marriage can be invalid, despite having the appearance of being valid.

- A sacramental marriage takes place between two baptized Christians.

- The goal of the annulment process is to provide clarity and healing.

QUESTIONS FOR REFLECTION

1. What are the reasons I would or would not start the annulment process?

2. Is it possible that revisiting the dating, engagement, and married periods of my relationship with my ex-spouse might shed some light on why my marriage failed?

3. Am I apprehensive about what might be the outcome if I go through the annulment process? If so, why?

CHAPTER TWO

"A Time to Keep, and a Time to Cast Away"

Debunking Common Myths and Addressing Pope Francis' Changes

It was September 8, 2015, and the mainstream media was loudly buzzing on all the airwaves, broadcasting the news that Pope Francis had just declared sweeping changes to the annulment process that were shaking up the Church. I turned on my television and tuned in to CNN's midday show just in time to hear their report on it. The changes were inaccurately written out as bullet points on the screen:

- "Annulments must be free and completed within 45 days"
- "Eliminate second review by cleric before marriage nullified"
- "Gives bishops ability to fast-track and grant annulments".

I shook my head in disappointment as I read those bullet points. One was absolutely false: annulments do not have to be free or completed within forty-five days. The others were worded in deliberately misleading ways that would create a lot of misunderstanding. "Here we go again!" I thought to myself. The folks at CNN had just succeeded in bringing ample amounts of confusion to people all over the world by misreporting what Pope Francis' changes actually were. I was stunned by just how badly they could get it wrong, but not really surprised at their careless reporting.

The worst result of it all, in my opinion, would be the varied, strong reactions that would ripple through the Catholic community because of all the erroneous and slanted reports. Some would be angry, others would celebrate, but beyond doubt there would be widespread confusion that would have Church officials tripping over themselves to clarify. Before that day was over, I, being a writer who serves the divorced Catholic community, had received several emails asking questions about what had happened. Some wanted clarification, and many were stating their renewed interest in taking a second look at the annulment process because of these new changes.

All I knew was that I definitely had my work cut out for me now, and I wasn't even a Church official. It was going to be a long haul in this department. So, as we continue our conversation here and dive into the controversial waters of Pope Francis' changes to the annulment process, I believe it's critical to underscore his motivation behind the changes. There has been so much finger-pointing and divisiveness surrounding his announcement that it's important to get back to the focal point: the pope made the changes out of pastoral concern. As Cindy Wooden wrote for the Catholic News Service the very day of the announcement: "Pope Francis said the changes in the annulment process were motivated by 'concern for the salvation of souls,' and particularly 'charity and mercy' toward those who feel alienated from the church because of their marriage situations and the perceived complexity of the church's annulment process."[2]

Many people, especially within the Church, criticize Pope Francis because they believe his "Who am I to judge?" perspective is paving the way for all sorts of errors. To be fair, if someone uses "Who am I to judge?" as a way of turning a blind eye to something obviously immoral, that is a problem. But, in my estimation, that is not what Pope Francis is doing, and it certainly was not his intention in his administrative changes to the annulment process. Pope Francis is working to break down the walls between Catholics who feel estranged from the Faith and their parish communities.

---

2. Cindy Wooden, "Pope Simplifies Annulment Process, Asks That It Be Free of Charge," Catholic News Service, September 8, 2015.

As he so aptly expresses it, churches should be "the field hospital after the battle." And as anyone knows who has gone through it, divorce is one of the fiercest battles of all.

My goal with this chapter is to debunk the most common myths about the annulment process and make a few clarifications about the changes Pope Francis made. The pope implemented these changes with the hopes of streamlining the process within the Church and making the whole thing more approachable by Catholics who otherwise didn't think they had a chance.

First Stop: Annulment Lingo

One big reason why there is so much confusion surrounding the annulment process is because of the improper use of terms. The CNN anchors who reported Pope Francis' changes used the word "nullified." This is incorrect. The annulment process does not "nullify" a marriage. Either the marriage was valid or it was invalid. If it was valid, the process will determine and declare that the two spouses are still bound to each other regardless of a civil divorce. If it was invalid, it will be declared so, and the spouses are not bound to each other.

A surprising stumbling block is the word "annulment" itself. Let's use a different term so you can have a clearer understanding of what it actually is. Let's use the more defining term, "decree of invalidity." A decree of invalidity (also referred to as a "decree of nullity") is precisely what it sounds like: it is a decree that states that one who has gone through the annulment process did not have a valid marriage and is now free to marry. This is usually a letter the petitioner (the former spouse initiating the annulment process) and the respondent (the other ex-spouse) receive at the end of the process, if it is determined that, indeed, no valid marriage existed. That letter is what people typically refer to as an annulment. An "annulment" does not "nullify" a valid marriage — only death can do that. It declares that a valid marriage did not take place.

This may bring up a very important question, one that many people ask almost immediately: *If I receive a decree of invalidity, does that mean my marriage never existed?*

How Dare You Say My Marriage Never Existed!

I was attending an annulment seminar about fifteen years ago that was being given by an outstanding priest and canon lawyer, Father Bob. In a room of about fifty attendees, there was one gentleman sitting toward the front of the room who was clearly agitated. Father Bob had only been speaking for about ten minutes when this gentleman stood up and interrupted him. With a furious tone and shaking his finger at the priest, he shouted, "I don't care about all this nonsense you are talking about! I want to know if you're going to tell me my marriage never existed!" This gentleman was experiencing righteous anger and indignation, having been betrayed by his wife of twenty-eight years, who had divorced him and abandoned their family. He, too, had fallen prey to this particular myth about the annulment process.

Lots of people worry about this same thing and feel angry and distraught at the belief that receiving a decree of invalidity might mean their marriage was all for nothing — all those years of working hard and raising a family, all the good moments, all the struggles, all the love and all the pain. Does a decree of invalidity mean none of it counted? Especially for people who were married for thirty years or more (and there are many), the idea that all of it could be considered a total sham is beyond heartbreaking.

If you have concerns in this area, please know that receiving a decree of invalidity does *not* mean your marriage relationship never existed. The Church recognizes that you lived in society under the assumption that your marriage was valid. There is even a technical term for this in canon law: it is called a "putative" (from the Latin for "supposed") marriage. You had children, a house, a dog, a mini-van, etc. You had a *real* relationship that was witnessed by society at large, and nothing can take that away. The decree of invalidity declares that the *bond* was not valid, meaning that, although you lived together as husband and wife, your marriage was not an unbreakable covenant between you, your spouse, and God.

The United States Conference of Catholic Bishops (USCCB) states the answer to this question in this way:

It means that a marriage that was thought to be valid civilly and canonically was in fact not valid according to Church law. A declaration of invalidity does not deny that a relationship existed. It simply states that the relationship was missing something that the Church requires for a valid marriage.[3]

What to Keep, What to Throw Away

Now that we have a better understanding of what the annulment process is and what the terms mean, let's start throwing away the myths. The more we are freed from the lies and misinformation, the more we can focus on what we can keep: the truth.

Myth No. 1: "An Annulment Is Just a 'Get Out of Jail Free' Card"

The annulment process is not available just so divorcees who subscribe to the notion that marriages are disposable can be issued a "Get Out of Jail Free" card and get remarried. This is not the Catholic Church making divorce palatable or sanctioning the culture's lack of respect for the integrity of marriage. I would say the annulment process is more like relationship rehab. It's all about coming clean, making peace with the past, and discovering your new direction in life. As you consider whether or not the annulment process is right for you, I strongly encourage you to approach it with the desire of finding the new direction God has in store for you.

Myth No. 2: "The Annulment Process Is Just a Moneymaker for the Church"

Officially, there is no cost for the annulment process. When tribunals do request a fee, most ask only for an amount that would cover their basic administrative costs, and that amount varies from diocese to diocese. Any funds received by the tribunal are used to pay salaries, cover office supplies, and so on. People have paid anything from nothing to $1,000. But what seems to be true for most dioceses — and it certainly was in my case in the diocese

---

3. Church Teachings, "Annulments (Declarations of Nullity)," ForYourMarriage.org.

of Bridgeport, Connecticut — is that if you are enduring financial hardships, the tribunal will either reduce the amount for you or not charge you at all. If you are worried that you will not be able to afford the fee, the best thing you can do is call the tribunal and discuss your financial hardship with someone that can help you work out an arrangement.

After my divorce, I struggled mightily with my finances, as so many newly divorced people do. I worked two jobs just to cover my expenses, and even then I was destitute. I had no expendable cash, and money was extremely tight for quite some time. I was suffering emotionally, spiritually, and physically. The priest who was giving me spiritual direction encouraged me to apply for the annulment process so that I could find some peace and move on from this terrible period in my life. I followed his prompts, but when I saw the fee associated with getting an annulment, I dropped it all like a hot potato. The fee was not exorbitant or unreasonable, but it was a fee — more money I had to shell out — and I just could not afford it, so I walked away.

Later on, in my post-divorce years, I was able to reapply for an annulment, and they allowed me to make payments that were affordable on my income. I was even told that if I absolutely could not afford the cost, they would waive the fee altogether.

This was just my experience, but across the board, tribunals are willing to work with petitioners. In fact, in a rather bold move, in 2014 the Diocese of Cleveland eliminated all fees associated with the annulment process. For petitioners already in the process and awaiting a final decision, remaining balances would be waived. This was a huge step toward bringing more Catholics back to the Church and a trend that I sincerely hope will be followed by other dioceses and archdioceses. Bishop Richard Lennon said the decision was made to "encourage greater participation in the life of the church" by Catholics in "irregular marital situations, such as divorce and remarriage," citing Pope Francis' efforts to encourage ministry to divorced and separated Catholics "so that they do not feel excluded from the mercy of God."[4]

---

4. Catholic News Agency, June 9, 2014.

This is a welcome relief for many Catholic men and women who struggle with the legal expenses of a civil divorce and making ends meet on a single income. It is a gesture of welcoming to Catholics who feel alienated from the Church because of their circumstances. It also promotes the idea that, as Pope Francis so aptly stated, the Church should be a field hospital welcoming those in need of healing — including especially the abundance of healing to be found in the annulment process.

For a long time, some Catholics have contended that the annulment process was just a moneymaker for the Catholic Church, as if the hierarchy was not truly concerned with the healing of the petitioner, but only with receiving a check. I have heard many angry divorced Catholics complain this was just one of several reasons they stayed away from the annulment process. It breaks my heart to know this falsehood is keeping people from finding the peace and healing they need, especially those who have remarried without a decree of invalidity. As more dioceses take steps to make the process affordable and accessible to all, perhaps those who have avoided the process will give it another chance.

Myth No. 3: "The Annulment Process Drags on for Years and Years"

As stated before, the annulment process is not simply administrative, where a staff processes forms and mails letters. It is a serious procedure in which a team of canon lawyers carefully reads and debates the information you and your witnesses have provided. Because their decision will directly impact the rest of your life, it is not something that should be taken lightly, and for this reason it makes sense that it would take more than a few weeks to be resolved.

However, it is true that some cases have taken twenty-four months or more to be resolved, and it's important to understand why this might happen:

- There may be a high number of cases ahead of yours that are waiting to be processed.

- Other complexities may exist — for instance, if you have more than one marriage to investigate. As an example, if a person wants to be received into the Church via the RCIA (Rite of Christian Initiation of Adults) but has been married multiple times, the tribunal must investigate all of the marriages to be able to come to a determination and possibly declare each previous marriage null.

- The process will be impacted by the length of time it takes you and your witnesses to fill out and submit your paperwork to the tribunal. Believe it or not, this plays a big role in reducing or increasing the amount of time the process will take, and more often than not it is the reason why some cases take so long. Many people drag their feet during the paperwork process, and doing so will delay the resolution of your case. A good rule of thumb is to encourage your witnesses to fill out their questionnaires as completely and promptly as possible, and for you to do the same. This will help things roll along in a much smoother manner.

But here is another very important fact: despite the sincere diligence of the petitioner, many annulment cases have gotten "stuck" in the system for various reasons, and this causes a lot of frustration. It can also make the annulment process a painful experience for the one who has done everything within his or her power to keep the case moving forward. This was a motivating factor for Pope Francis when he announced his changes to the annulment process back in September 2015, one of those changes being creating a "fast track" process for individuals who fell into specific circumstances.

In his apostolic letter *Mitis Iudex Dominus Iesus* ("The Lord Jesus, the Gentle Judge"), Pope Francis describes the circumstances under which this briefer process may take place:[5]

---

5. Art. 14 § 1.

- "the defect of faith which can generate simulation of consent or error that determines the will;"
- "a brief conjugal cohabitation;"
- "an abortion procured to avoid procreation;"
- "an obstinate persistence in an extra conjugal relationship at the time of the wedding or immediately following it;"
- "the deceitful concealment of sterility, or grave contagious illness, or children from a previous relationship, or incarcerations;"
- "a cause of marriage completely extraneous to married life, or consisting of the unexpected pregnancy of the woman;"
- "physical violence inflicted to extort consent,"
- "the defect of the use of reason, which is proved by medical documents, etc."

The Holy Father has instituted these changes to help alleviate some of the pain and frustration that might arise out of a long wait for a decision on a person's case. Other significant changes Pope Francis has instituted are:

- Requiring only a single judgment of invalidity. Usually, a judgment in the first instance and second instance was required, but Pope Francis eliminated the requirement of the second court judgment. He did not eliminate the court itself, for it is still there in case one would like to appeal their decision; he just eliminated the requirement on regular cases.
- Bishops are approved to be judges and appoint their own assistants. While bishops were always the ultimate judge for their diocese, this new mandate appoints them as active judges on annulment cases.

Myth No. 4: "The Annulment Process Is Mandatory"
The annulment process is only mandatory if you want to remarry

after divorce. Many people choose not to remarry and, therefore, are under no obligation to go through the process.

Myth No. 5: "The Annulment Process Is an Undue Imposition on Friends and Family"
A few years ago, I was giving a talk on the annulment process at my parish, and during the Q and A session at the end, one of the parishioners shared that a relative of hers had asked her to be a witness in her annulment case. She agreed, but when she reviewed the dozen or so questions on the questionnaire, she felt it was too intrusive and declined to participate.

I can certainly understand that initial reaction to something so personal, especially when you are asked to provide information about someone else. But, as I pointed out to her, it's important to understand *why* those questions are being asked of a friend or relative. It's not because the tribunal is looking for gossip or dirty laundry; they need to have a well-rounded picture of what happened, and often the witnesses' testimony fills in many blanks to help create a more complete picture.

Take, for example, Jeanine's story. Jeanine's daughter, Meg, had been married for six years and had a three-year-old son. Because they lived in close proximity to each other, Jeanine would watch her grandson during the week while Meg went to work. Jeanine began noticing strange things about her daughter that led her to suspect she was being physically abused by her husband. Meg would always wear long-sleeved, high neck shirts, even in the sweltering summer heat. She never wanted to stay long or spend too much time talking about things. She never brought her husband around with her, and she always seemed impatient and uptight. When Jeanine finally confronted Meg with her suspicions, Meg stopped coming over and found a different babysitter for her son. As it turns out, she was indeed hiding physical abuse from her mother. These are examples of important details that can add to the bigger picture the canon lawyers need to create and really help them detect what the problems were in the relationship.

Witnesses and their testimonies are an integral part of the annulment process, which is why you should select yours carefully.

A good candidate to ask to be a witness would be someone who has known both you and your ex-spouse well as a couple. It doesn't matter whether a witness is a friend or relative, but very often witnesses are family members.

Myth No. 6: "The Annulment Process Will Not Proceed Without Your Ex-spouse's Participation"

Your ex-spouse is given the opportunity to participate, which he or she may either accept or refuse. If your ex-spouse refuses to participate, this will not stop the proceedings in most cases.[6] It will simply mean less information for the canon lawyers to go by.

Myth No. 7: "Getting an Annulment Will Make My Children Illegitimate"

Many people who have come to understand what the annulment process really does are afraid that it means their children will now be considered illegitimate. I have seen terror in people's eyes over this question: *If the marriage wasn't valid, does that mean the children were somehow invalid as well?* This is definitely a myth. Canon 1137 states: "The children conceived or born of a valid or putative marriage are legitimate." Rest assured that children from any marriage that was presumed to be valid, but later defined through the annulment process as not valid, are not considered illegitimate.

Myth No. 8: "It's Okay to Date and Make Plans to Marry During the Annulment Process"

This is actually one of the biggest myths out there, and one that can bring a lot of complications to your life for two major reasons.

First, because you need to know if you are free to date or be married again, and you can only be certain of this by going through the annulment process and receiving a decree of invalidity. Why? Because the Church assumes all marriages are valid unless proven otherwise by the annulment process. What's at stake here is the fact that there is no guarantee you will receive

---

6. There are some special circumstances that require an ex-spouse's response.

that decree, so the Church recommends that you do not get into dating relationships or make any plans to remarry before receiving an annulment. This way, you will not find yourself in the painful position of being in a new relationship, yet not free to marry. This is the Church's way of looking out for you and helping you avoid future mistakes.

Second, your heart really needs time to heal, and that doesn't happen quickly after a divorce. Being in a new relationship doesn't heal your heart, either, but actually pushes aside the pain and leaves it unattended. It then becomes emotional baggage that you will drag with you from relationship to relationship. This is no way to begin a new commitment to love with someone. The best way to do that is to take the time to heal properly and make sure your heart is ready to be given away when the time is right.

The period of time it takes to go through the annulment process is actually a precious gift to you — a specific period of time you will never have again — and should be used for reflection and improvement. Since no one is perfect, this time of waiting for an answer is the perfect time to start polishing your interior and exterior self. In my own experience, I found the time I had to wait for an answer became a period of my life that gave me the opportunity to reflect on what had happened and use it to improve myself in several ways.

For one thing, I was able to accept the fact that, although I didn't want the divorce and fought for my marriage, I was not a perfect spouse, and I contributed to the divorce. This was difficult but very necessary, because it allowed me to stop being a victim. I put an end to the blame game, and that was a critical step in being able to move forward to my new life.

I was becoming overwhelmed by the "what if's." *What if I don't receive a decree of invalidity? Then what?* That was an unbearable thought process during the waiting period, so I had to learn to trust God and his plan. I knew that the decision was in his hands, and that there was nothing more I could do except let go. This was a difficult but fruitful exercise, and if you learn to do this you will benefit from it all your life.

I also made note of the fact that, if I was able to date in the future, I would need to make much better choices. The annulment process brought to light many poor decisions I had made before, and I knew that had to change. I took the time to really reflect on the flaws I had brought into the marriage and worked on being a better person. I needed to work on patience, forgiveness, maturity, and communication.

Is Getting an Annulment a Sin?

There are some Catholics who claim that the annulment process is merely a sham; that it is just another legal process that fakes people into believing they can dispose of a marriage they're tired of and go find a new one without any eternal spiritual consequences. Are they correct?

In some cases, *yes*.

It is true, unfortunately, that some Catholics use the annulment process for their own dishonest intentions. They divorce their spouses, abandon their families, and after the civil side of things has been settled, they file for the annulment process, often lying about the factors they say caused their marriages to "fail."

In other cases, the abandoned spouse is already hurting over losing a marriage they were willing to fight for. Finding themselves handed a decree of invalidity that states their marriage bond was never valid is beyond unjust and insulting. For anyone in this situation, I am sorry this has happened to you, and I know you have suffered greatly.

However, there is an important fact that critics of the annulment process don't take into consideration: despite the fact that some people deliberately misuse the process for selfish purposes, this important process within the Church is still a valid and necessary one. As is the case with many good and important things (including marriage itself), just because the system can be abused does not make it a bad system.

For a lot of marriages, there really was an impediment to bringing a valid marriage into being. This is something that can be very difficult to accept, especially for a spouse who was forced into a divorce. In my own experience, I did not want to be divorced. I was willing to forgive everything (and there was a lot, believe me) and work on saving my marriage. But the no-fault divorce laws made that a moot point. It was only after going through the annulment process that I was able to recognize the obstacles that had truly existed in our relationship. I could then see quite clearly that our marriage was never valid. It was a bitter pill to swallow, precisely because I was so vehemently against divorce, but the truth I discovered allowed me to heal and move forward.

Moreover, the annulment process by and large is administered by canon lawyers, both clergy and laypeople. Their sole desire is to complete an honest, objective, and thorough investigation of a marriage so as to determine whether or not the couple had a valid marriage bond. The team of canon lawyers involved in deciding annulment cases will always include a "Defender of the Bond." This person is a member of the team of canon lawyers whose role is to play devil's advocate in defense of the couple's union. These people take what they're doing seriously and rely on the Holy Spirit's guidance, because they know their own eternal salvation hangs in the balance of the decisions they make, as well as the salvation of those for whom they are making the decision.

An Apostolic Tradition

History also reveals the importance the Church has placed on the annulment process, because it goes way back — in fact, all the way back to the time of the apostles. Saint Paul allowed the dissolution of a non-Christian marriage (two unbaptized persons or one baptized Christian and one unbaptized person) in favor of the Faith, meaning, if one spouse wanted to practice Christianity and the other did not, their marriage was declared null, and they were free to marry someone else. Why did he do this?

At that time, many pagans were converting to Christianity, which caused couples to be at odds. Saint Paul, in his wisdom, knew that Christ must come first in a person's life, so if one spouse believed in Christ and the other was against him, the marriage bond could be dissolved by a new sacramental bond so that the believing spouse could live out his or her faith in Christ (cf. 1 Cor 7:12–15). This is known today as the Pauline Privilege, and it cannot be used if it is the baptized spouse who "departs." If the unbaptized spouse is willing to remain in the marriage, and is not hostile to the Christian faith of the other spouse, the marriage cannot be dissolved except by death, as according to Canon 1141.

Overall, the annulment process is there to help a person devastated by divorce by offering the opportunity to sort out what happened, recognize the poor choices that were made, make peace with the past, and finally move forward in life with a clear and distinct direction. This can happen even when the decision is that the marriage was valid.

QUICK POINTS RECAP

- The term "decree of invalidity" is more accurate than the word "annulment."

- The Church wholeheartedly recognizes marriage relationships as real and important, even when the annulment process determines there was no valid marriage bond in a particular case.

- The annulment process is not a "Catholic divorce" or "get out of jail free" card; it is a determination of whether or not a valid bond existed.

- It is not a "moneymaker" for the Church, especially since Pope Francis' request that all dioceses make the annulment process free of charge or significantly reduce costs.

- The typical length of time for the annulment process is about sixteen months, start to finish. It might go on longer if the petitioner becomes unresponsive, does not submit the paperwork in a timely manner, or there is some other deficiency.

- The annulment process is only mandatory for those who wish to remarry in the Church.

- The testimony of family and friends as witnesses holds great value in the annulment process.

- Your ex-spouse is given the opportunity to participate in the process, but if declined, it will still proceed.

- The annulment questionnaire's very personal nature serves the purpose of providing as much detail to the canon lawyers as possible so that they can make an informed decision.

- Dating and engagement should be reserved for after the annulment process, when you have received the decision that states whether or not you are free to marry.

QUESTIONS FOR REFLECTION

1. What has been the most helpful aspect of this chapter, and why?

2. What are my thoughts on the annulment questionnaire?

3. After reading this chapter, do I now feel that going through the annulment process might be a good thing for me? Why or why not?

CHAPTER THREE

"A Time to Embrace, and a Time to Refrain from Embracing"

A Special Note to Divorced and Civilly Remarried Catholics

Everyone loves witnessing the joy and excitement of two people who are in love and engaged to be married, especially me. Watching a man and a woman being joined together as husband and wife and setting off on their lifetime adventure as a new family is quite moving. When you commit your life to someone else, it's so important to begin your life together by setting yourselves up for success. Unfortunately, there are many "cultural myths" out there that warp our perception of what starting married life out on the right foot actually looks like. These myths may seem like good ideas, but they can actually become obstacles in the way of living a happy life together.

For example, my friend Shane and his beautiful fiancée, Emma, were a wonderful couple who seemed absolutely perfect for each other. I didn't know beforehand, but Emma had been through a terrible divorce three years before, and in meeting and falling in love with Shane, she was elated to have been granted a second chance at married life and having a family. Many friends, including myself, gathered one Sunday for their engagement party, where a very eye-opening conversation took place and personally made me worried for them.

Since none of their family members were local, one of the party guests asked where the wedding would take place. The bride-to-be responded, "We're actually going to have three weddings!"

Surprised laughter and applause filled the room. "Shane's parents are in Indiana and my parents are in Florida, and my mother insists on us getting married down there. But traveling is hard on Shane's parents because of their ages, so we're going to have a wedding in both locations. They'll be small weddings, but it's worth it because all our family will be able to attend."

"When is the third wedding?" someone asked. The room hushed.

"It's actually next week!" Emma replied with a loving look at Shane. "We've been waiting for my annulment to come through, but it doesn't look like that will happen anytime soon. We just want to be together and make it official, so we'll be married on Friday evening by a justice of the peace at that beautiful courtyard with the fountain downtown. Then, we'll have the 'real' weddings later, after the annulment comes through." The bride and groom kissed and polite applause followed, but I actually felt sad. Why? Because, I wanted the best for my friends: to see them married and living happily ever after. But what Emma had just described was a recipe for disaster.

You see, although Shane and Emma were being very generous in trying to accommodate their family members and include them in their plans, they were actually buying into two dangerous myths: the "it's just a ceremony" myth and the "a civil wedding is fine until the annulment comes through" myth. In doing so, they were setting themselves up for some serious problems and heartache in the future.

Let's address the obvious first: once a couple exchanges their vows and sacramentally forges their marriage bond, it *cannot* be repeated. They cannot re-marry themselves after they have forged this bond. Once they are married, they are married. So, you can't really have three weddings. But this actually is the least of the problems.

The greater concern, as previously discussed, is that since a divorced Catholic is still considered married to her ex-spouse if she has not received a decree of invalidity from a diocesan tribunal stating that her marriage was invalid, she cannot validly marry in the Catholic Church or anywhere else. Marrying someone else when her prior marriage is considered valid would constitute *adultery*. In that case, she would not be able to receive the sacraments. And since getting married by a justice of the peace can never bring a valid marriage into being due to its lack of canonical form, doing this in advance of a "real" wedding would not validate them as a married couple any more than a church wedding would before receiving a decree of invalidity.

Probably the greatest concern here, however, is that there is absolutely no guarantee she will receive a decree of invalidity. This means that getting married before receiving that final decision, or making plans for marriage without having that decree of invalidity, is a *huge* gamble. If the tribunal determines her prior marriage is indeed valid, her happy new marriage becomes extremely complicated because, in the end, she is still married to her "former" spouse.

And that tends to be the tipping point for a couple in this situation. Their options now are either to stay in an adulterous marriage and be prohibited from receiving the sacraments, or live as brother and sister in order to be able to receive the sacraments. Either way, it becomes an extremely difficult and painful situation.

The number of couples who are divorced, civilly remarried, and wanting to be in full communion with the Church but unable to do so has become a bit of a crisis over the years. Sometimes it is due to the fact that they just don't understand the consequences of getting married without receiving a decree of invalidity. Sometimes it's because the couple just doesn't want to wait. Regardless, this predicament leaves many couples who want to be in full communion with the Church feeling, first, condemned, because they are now prohibited from receiving the sacraments; and second, doomed — because the only opportunity for them to receive the sacraments would be to separate or live with their spouse as brother and sister. That is why this chapter is titled, "A Time to Embrace, and a Time to Refrain from Embracing," because after going through a divorce, there really is a time to take a step back and abstain from entering into a new relationship.

Aside from not knowing if you're free to date because you don't have a decree of invalidity, healing from a traumatic event such as divorce not only takes time but also effort on your part. I myself went through this challenging period, and I can tell you firsthand that it's very difficult to give your heart to someone else when it's filled with anger and resentment toward your ex-spouse and anyone else who played a role in the failure of your marriage. People tend to go right from the ugly scene of divorce straight into the arms of someone new, and they drag all that baggage with them. Sure, having someone new who finds you attractive, interesting, and nice to be around is a powerful and addictive feeling. It may even convince you that this new relationship is exactly what you need to heal from the pain and move forward, but it never works that way. If you're not healed, you will bring the same problems you had in your prior marriage into your new relationship. And honestly, is it really fair to that new person in your life to offer him or her a heart that is still steeped in anger and resentment?

The time for preparing your heart for a future relationship — one that you want to be successful, of course — is during at least the first few years after going through your divorce. This is also the perfect time to initiate the annulment process, which, as we've discussed, can play a major role in helping you heal.

But I Just Want to Be Happy!

A year ago, I met a wonderful gentleman named Jack at one of my husband's work events. Jack was in this very predicament. We were sitting next to each other tasting small bowls of chili for a chili-cook-off contest, and since Jack was extremely nice and very personable, our conversation took off right away. Inevitably, he asked what I did for a living, and when I told him I was an author whose focus was serving the divorced Catholic community, he responded with, "Oh, I used to be a divorced Catholic." I listened to him relay his sad story of losing his marriage. The story ended with, "And then I fell in love with _____, and we didn't want to wait all that time for me to get an annulment, so we got married. Now, we go to _____ church and are pretty happy."

I asked him, "Do you ever miss being Catholic?"

He replied with a shrug, "Yes, but I can't go back now." The look on his face was somewhat crestfallen.

"But you can!" I said, and then we were abruptly interrupted by the contest master of ceremonies announcing more contest information. Had I only had more time and more privacy with him, I would have tried to help him see that he could come back. *All Catholics are welcome to attend Mass*, even if they cannot receive the sacraments, and attending Mass is a great way to start things happening. Not only that, but the Church wants to help these couples resolve their situations so that they can at some point fully partake in the sacraments. As long as a person is willing, the clergy and lay-appointed parish leaders always work toward a resolution to the problem. People like Jack would just need to be willing to submit themselves to the process.

And that's yet another part of this problem. I've heard many people complain that they just want to be happy, and that the Church is being unfair: *What is so wrong about falling in love and getting married when you are already civilly divorced? Why are the Church's standards so high (too high, many will say) that the people who are just trying to get on with their lives after a horrendous experience should be penalized?*

I understand why people might feel this way, and because this is such a widespread complaint, I'd just like to offer some food for thought on this.

First, the Church's standards are specifically set in place to help us achieve the happiness we search for all our lives. These standards are not a jail cell: they're like a ladder that, with each step, leads you closer to your goal. Or think of them as a guard rail on a mountainous road that keeps your car from driving off the edge of a cliff, or a fence surrounding a playground near a busy city street that keeps the children playing happily without being in danger. These are just a few examples to illustrate how Jesus' teachings, which are upheld by the Catholic Church, are actually parameters to live by that will keep us safe and happy. When the Church tells us that we need to wait until the annulment process is complete and a declaration regarding validity or invalidity is made before getting married, she is actually looking out for our best interests, even if it seems really hard to wait. And it's just as much for our good (the good of our souls) when the Church asks a divorced and civilly remarried couple to refrain from the sacraments until their situation can be rectified.

If you are already in a civil marriage and want to rectify your situation so that you can be in full communion with the Church, that's wonderful. If you want to receive the sacraments, the Church asks that you and your spouse live as brother and sister until the validity of the first marriage can be determined. "I don't see how not being able to have sex with my spouse is a standard that will make me happy," you might be thinking. I understand why you feel this way. But if you think about it as a ladder, this one important step brings you closer to God, closer to the sacraments, closer to spending eternity in heaven. It's a sacrifice for a short period of time in exchange for an eternity in heaven.

Too often we consider happiness as something that only counts in this moment. Our perspective on finding happiness is that it should occur here and now. But when we think this way, we fail to consider the end result of choosing happiness in the moment. When you go through a divorce, the incredible pain and sadness you experience makes it easy to look for happiness in this moment because, of course, you want to rid yourself of those terrible feelings. This is precisely why people go out and search for someone new to love — but at what cost? The happiness they are looking for can only be found in Christ. So, if a relationship you want to have blocks your path to Christ because you're not able to receive the Eucharist, why would you tolerate that? Why would you let anything stand in the way of being one with Christ?

If you have been staying away from your parish because of a civil marriage, I encourage you to reflect upon that last point and search your heart to see if there is a way you can begin making your way back to Mass. And as far as not being able to receive the Eucharist, I have something very important to tell you.

You Are Not a Second-class Citizen

I am fully aware that many of you want to be in full communion with the Church but are unable to do so because you have been divorced and remarried without having gone through the annulment process and receiving a decree of invalidity. I know that many of you continue to come to Mass and respectfully do not approach the Eucharist but instead wait patiently in the pews. I commend you for setting this example of fidelity and respect for the Eucharist and the prescriptions of the Church. Not only are you doing what is right and appropriate despite what it costs you, but you are also setting a very good example for others. And believe me, others take notice.

Since the Synod on the Family concluded in October 2015, your particular impediment has gained global attention and is debated in the public square in ways that can be totally confusing and make it sound as if the Church is treating you unfairly. And so, I'd like to cut through all the noisy voices and heated arguments to offer you a simple explanation that will help you understand what exactly is going on.

Many people believe the Church's standards regarding the reception of the Eucharist by divorced and civilly remarried Catholics are unfair and harshly discriminatory, but as previously noted, it's actually a parameter put in place to help you. As I mentioned at the beginning of chapter 2, the media have seriously complicated this discussion by misreporting details about something they themselves don't even understand. They've succeeded in spinning this debate into a sort of "human rights" issue, leading many divorced and civilly remarried Catholics to believe they are being treated unfairly, as if they were second-class citizens. I assure you, nothing could be further from the truth.

The truth about who can and cannot receive the Eucharist is actually quite simple: *anyone* (married, never married, widowed, divorced, religious) who is not in the state of grace is prohibited from receiving Holy Communion (*Catechism of the Catholic Church*, 1385). What causes one to not be in a state of grace? Mortal sin.

Since we've come all this way together so far, let's have a frank discussion about that pesky little word "sin." No one likes to hear that word, and society has pretty much convinced everyone that it doesn't exist. But the truth is, it does exist, and we are *all* subject to it, not just divorced and civilly remarried Catholics. As a married woman, I am subject to it, the pope is, the saints were — it's part of the human condition. But the goal of acknowledging our sins is not to discourage us or make us feel like losers. Acknowledging our sins is actually ... medicinal! When we acknowledge our sins, it helps us become better people, because it causes us to improve ourselves by working to overcome them. Therein lies the beauty of the Sacrament of Reconciliation: when we confess our sins, our slate is wiped clean and we get to begin again.

But part of this process is also acknowledging *there are consequences to sin.* Imagine it this way: going to confession is like pulling a nail out of a piece of wood. The nail (sin) has been removed, but there is still a visible hole (consequences) left in the wood. So while we all have to acknowledge the various consequences for our sins, the particular consequence for being civilly remarried after divorce is the need to refrain from receiving the sacraments until your situation has been rectified, or to live as brother and sister so that you can receive the sacraments.

Being divorced in and of itself is not necessarily a sin because many spouses who end up divorced were forced into it. Therefore, they did not commit a sin. But contracting a second marriage outside the Church without receiving a declaration of invalidity for any previous marriage does put one in a state of mortal sin because the first marriage is still considered to be valid. This would apply to both spouses, no matter who initiated the divorce.

You Are Not Alone

The same standards also apply to cohabiting couples who are not married, persons in same-sex unions, and anyone else who is living in an irregular life situation. But remember, it goes for me too. It goes for everyone. We *all* must approach the Eucharist, this holy sacrament, this miracle Christ gives us, with the highest regard and the utmost humility so that we do not bring condemnation upon ourselves. The Church wants to protect us and preserve the necessary respect for the Eucharist.

The Takeaway

The bottom line is, if you are a divorced and civilly remarried Catholic, this mandate is not intended to single you out and ostracize you. It is about protecting you from further grave sin and encouraging you to resolve your circumstances so you may receive the Eucharist worthily. This is not something new in the Church. The early Christians were admonished to prepare themselves properly to receive the Eucharist. In the fourth century, Saint John Chrysostom, one of the Fathers of the Church, urged the faithful to approach the Eucharist not just with clean hands and clean clothes but with "clean souls."[7]

If you are a divorced and civilly remarried Catholic who feels the call to come home to the Catholic Church, please know that God has not abandoned you. Neither has the Catholic Church. All it takes is some action on your part, and here are the steps you can take:

1. Talk about your desire to begin coming back to the Church with your spouse and discuss what this would look like in your specific situation. Are you both willing to abstain from sexual intimacy in order to receive the sacraments? If not, are you at least willing to begin going to Mass and remaining in the pew during Communion? Beginning with just coming back to Mass is a great way to start paving the way for future steps.

2. Make an appointment with your pastor or any knowledgeable priest, and take the time to discuss your situation with him. When he knows the details of your specific situation, he is better equipped to offer his own insights and recommendations.

3. Go to the Sacrament of Reconciliation and confess the sin of adultery. Don't let that little word "sin" make you feel anything but normal, like the rest of us sinners, and get ready to feel refreshed when you leave the confessional! It's a common phenomenon to feel as if the weight of the world has been lifted from you after going to confession.

---

7. Roberto de la Vega, *Eucharist Through the Centuries* (Circle Press, July 1998).

4. Ask your pastor to help you begin the annulment process. He will likely connect you with a parish case assistant (something I will tell you more about in the next chapter), and you can begin the paperwork and set the wheels in motion.

I enthusiastically encourage you to stay focused on the fact that, no matter how complicated your situation might seem, there is no obstacle that cannot be overcome if your heart is open and humble. There will be so much joy and many incredible blessings when you open yourself to God's will in your life. His grace is already at work.

QUICK POINTS RECAP

- Once a couple exchanges their vows and sacramentally forges their marriage bond, it cannot be repeated.

- A divorced Catholic is still considered married to his former spouse if he has not received a decree of invalidity. Therefore, he cannot validly marry in the Catholic Church or anywhere else. Marrying someone else when his prior marriage is considered valid would constitute adultery.

- Healing from a traumatic event such as divorce not only takes time but also effort, which is why it is best to take some time for yourself in the first few years after your divorce to rebuild and heal before you consider getting into a new relationship.

- *Anyone* (married, never married, widowed, divorced, religious) who is not in the state of grace is prohibited from receiving Holy Communion (*Catechism of the Catholic Church*, 1385).

- If you are a divorced and civilly remarried Catholic, this mandate is not intended to ostracize you. It is about protecting you from further grave sin and encouraging you to resolve your circumstances so that you may receive the Eucharist worthily.

QUESTIONS FOR REFLECTION

1. If I am a divorced and civilly remarried Catholic: Are there any specific issues that stand in the way of my coming back to Mass or beginning the annulment process? If so, what are they?

2. How does my spouse feel about the possibility of my going through the annulment process? What are his/her reasons for this?

3. What would be the best resolution for my situation? Why?

CHAPTER FOUR

"A Time to Break Down, and a Time to Build Up"

A Step-by-Step Walk Through the Annulment Process

I remember quite vividly the day my annulment questionnaire arrived in the mail. I was getting ready to go for an afternoon run when I checked the mailbox and found the large, yellow envelope. Because I was motivated to keep the annulment ball rolling, but really had no idea what to expect from this part of the process, I ripped into the envelope and pulled out a thick set of papers stapled together. After flipping past the first few pages, I began to read the questions. *Ugh!* I flipped through more pages and saw this was not something I would be able to complete in half an hour. These answers would be essays and would require a lot of pondering on my failed relationship with my ex-spouse.

As I continued to read, I began to feel the sorrow, which I had tried so hard to leave behind, welling up in my chest. I promptly opened the bottom drawer of my desk, dropped the questionnaire into it, kicked it closed with my foot, and walked out the door to go on my run. That document stayed right there in that drawer for a solid two weeks, because I knew I had to mentally prepare myself for this exercise.

I can honestly say that when I look back on this part of my experience with the annulment process, I don't remember it as some horrible event in my life. I have no regrets about chronicling the dating, engagement, and marriage phases of my relationship with my ex-spouse or writing out the details of episodes that were very painful to me. Actually, for me, that entire exercise was a huge relief. I finally got to tell someone in my own words about all the terrible things that had happened to me. It was critical for me to do this, and it had such a tremendous impact on my life going forward.

If you look at the questionnaire from a merely superficial perspective, it's easy to conclude that it is an unnecessary intrusion into the private details of your relationship — that it's *too* personal. But if you step back for a moment and think about it, marriage itself is *extremely* personal. The decision the tribunal is trying to make is directly related to the personal relationship you had with your former spouse, so it wouldn't make sense for them to ask superficial questions and merely gloss over the details that really matter because they didn't want to get "too personal." Their decision will have a direct impact on the rest of your life, so it stands to reason that the questions being asked have to be of a very personal nature.

My friend Rose Sweet, who is an annulment consultant and assists people going through their annulments, shares a personal experience she had working with a petitioner:

> *Sometimes invalidity is easy to prove when both parties respond, are honest, and there are strong witnesses who clearly focus on obvious grounds. But one of the biggest problems can result when grounds are of a much more subtle "psychological" nature known to very few outside the marriage — and the respondent does not participate. True story: The husband was overly attached to his wealthy and controlling mother to whom he gave primary emotional allegiance. To others he was outgoing, funny, and charming, but he was also an extreme narcissist, who, behind closed doors, was cruel, shaming, and abusive. He'd tried to force his wife to use pornography and indulge in twisted fantasy, mocking and belittling her for being a prude. When the kids came along, he taught them to belittle and mock their mother. When she had a miscarriage, he stayed on the golf course and told her to call her sister. There's much more. For many reasons, he was never able to form a true marriage bond with her and was incapable of authentic love — for anyone.*

She'd initially focused her annulment testimony on his faults. But in all those years, she'd rarely confided about his behaviors to anyone because of her shame. She'd felt trapped and was often depressed: divorce was a sin, and she had nowhere to go and no way to support herself.

"Who can testify to all you've said about him?" I'd asked. Very few wanted to get involved or say anything negative. Some family members still had a relationship with him. So as her advocate, I encouraged her to probe more deeply on her psychological issues and to find witnesses who could speak to those.

Her deepest healing began when she faced what she'd long avoided and even glossed over. Far from the perfect Catholic family she'd first described, she'd endured and normalized a high level of abuse starting in childhood. Her father and others had bullied and belittled her, with some sexually abusing her. Her mother had been passive, saying, "This is just how it is in a man's world, honey." There's more, but with these deep wounds, a temperament that avoids conflict at any cost, feeling trapped at home, and being swept away by his charms, she believed marriage was her only option for escape. But from the start, the marriage had been miserable, and very few knew it — or were willing to talk about what they might have seen or known.

Courageously, she began to identify her own character defects and admit she had used marriage as an escape and for financial support. That she had always feared him but had built a fantasy romance around him because she needed an out. Her consent to marriage had been damaged. Her siblings were able to testify to these things, and it helped the truth — at least on her side — get out and on record. And, eventually, she made a long, painfully honest, and beautiful confession as part of the process.

The bottom line here reveals an important truth in regard to this questionnaire: the more detail you provide, the deeper the enlightening and healing you are likely to experience through the annulment process. Questionnaires that are submitted with brief, simple responses are usually returned to the petitioner with a request for more detail because they do not contain enough of the information the canon lawyers need to make a final decision. This is another reason why a case could be delayed and take longer than necessary. If a petitioner is unwilling to provide more information, two things will happen: first, the petitioner misses out on the opportunity to experience that healing, personal growth, and closure; and second, usually the case will be dropped altogether.

Some people may not be good at expressing themselves through writing, and that can be part of the awkwardness. If you are having difficulty answering the questions, you can always ask for help from an auditor. Auditors will sit with you, ask you questions, and take your personal testimony. Then, they'll type out your answers and have you sign the document. If you have trouble writing out the answers, I recommend that you contact your local tribunal and ask them to provide you with an auditor.

If your particular tribunal does not have an auditor it can refer you to, I recommend looking for help from any of the various canon law groups that offer consulting on individual cases, such as Canon Law Professionals.com, or from individual consultants like Rose Sweet.

Don't let the questionnaire become a stumbling block. Part of the beauty of this process is in exposing your emotional wounds. While it can be difficult and painful, this is precisely what it takes to heal them. It's like any physical wound that requires medical attention: if you ignore it, it only gets worse. Observing and treating the wound is what allows the healing to begin — and that process can include a lot of pain at first. In that same sense, this is precisely what these questions are doing. Having the opportunity to say, "Yes, this terrible thing happened to me!" and being able to describe the details of that awful memory are the first steps in treating your emotional wounds. Is it painful? Yes. But it is a cleansing experience that allows you to acknowledge, accept, learn, and grow in ways that are difficult to find anywhere else.

A big part of healing from any traumatic life event is talking about it — getting it out of your heart and your head and into the open so you can take on a more objective viewpoint. As you prepare to start the annulment process, there is no doubt you need to be prepared to sit down and willingly revisit bad memories and painful experiences. Yet I want to assure you that in subjecting yourself to this often-painful process, you will also experience a lot of positive personal growth that can change you as a person. I found this aspect of the annulment process highly therapeutic, because I got to give my side of the story and share my pain with people who actually cared about what happened to me.

Yes, the Church Really Cares

You might wonder whether canon lawyers really "care" — and why. *Aren't they just doing their job?* Certainly, it is their job, but can you imagine wading through the ugliness of divorce stories, day after day, year after year, just to receive a mediocre paycheck? I once asked a personal friend who is a canon lawyer, Jacqui Rapp, specifically about this. What was it about her work that motivated her to get up each morning and get going? Her response was beautiful:

> *Bringing people back to the Communion table ... that is the end game for me. Knowing that because of what I do, people are reunited with the sacraments, people are set free from their issues, and they are willing and able to enter into healthier relationships if that's what they choose. This is the stuff that keeps you going, because this is hard work. Facing the annulment process day in and day out, you're dealing with people's destroyed lives. They've gone through horrible experiences, and then we have to read those horrible experiences ... it is difficult. So it's the fact that I'm instrumental in bringing them back to the table is what keeps me going.*

I certainly cannot speak for every person involved in deciding annulment cases, but I can say that, just as Jacqui said, most of those involved in this important work do their job because they want to help people discover the truth about their situation and recognize the mistakes they made so that they can go forth and make better choices in the future and, most importantly, heal from quite possibly the most devastating experience they will ever encounter.

Pre-Cana in Reverse

There is one point I'd like to make here that I haven't heard anyone ever talk about. In my opinion, this is the elephant in the room when it comes the annulment process: Why are these questions reserved for *after* a marriage has failed? Wouldn't it make more sense to ask these questions *before* a couple gets married?

The questionnaire contained inquiries about my childhood and my parents' marriage, and the same for my ex-husband. There were also questions about our career histories, our courtship, our wedding day. And perhaps the most insightful question, "What did it mean to you to be in love?" Having to answer that question in detail was like turning on a bright light in a dark room. Not only did I discover that my idea of love and marriage was very different from his, but I was able to identify certain immaturities that existed in my version of what being in love was all about. I can confidently share with you that those intensely personal answers I provided actually opened my eyes to the truth of what had happened.

Two aspects of the annulment questionnaire are particularly important for anyone preparing for marriage or considering the possibility of getting married again, after receiving a decree of invalidity: (1) the exploration of the childhood and family life of each partner and (2) detailed discussions about the couple's dating and engagement.

The first section offers insight into whether or not the future spouses have the right ideas about what marriage is. The questions focus on each person's religious upbringing; problems in the parents' marriage; any treatment for emotional, psychological, or psychiatric problems; any history of alcohol or drug abuse; and any history of physical, mental, or sexual abuse. The honest answers to these questions can begin to paint the bigger picture needed to know if one or both individuals are suitable for marriage.

The second set of questions reveals a lot about the maturity level of each partner before marriage and whether there might be any impediments already in existence. Many priests and therapists admit that too many couples preparing for marriage are ignorant of the fact that marriage is meant to be a permanent, exclusive, lifelong commitment that is open to new life.

In my case, I just couldn't understand why no one had asked me these questions *before* I got married. Couples who are taking their preparation for marriage seriously should be talking about more than just how they'll spend money and what their opinions on building a family are. I believe the substance they need can be found in these annulment questions — questions which, in my case and in the case of so many other couples, came too late.

In my humble opinion, the biggest problem we face today is that couples simply aren't marrying the way their grandparents and great-grandparents did. Society has placed many different kinds of pressures on singles and impressed ideas upon them that are not conducive to making a marriage last. And so, it is critical that going forward you understand the great need in properly preparing for marriage. I believe that the annulment questionnaire can help you make better choices in the future, should you decide to begin a new relationship and remarry.

Where Do I Even Begin?

I receive many emails from people who are feeling overwhelmed by the annulment process, and the question they ask most often is where to begin. As previously mentioned, the annulment process varies from diocese to diocese, but for the most part, the steps are the same. If you apply for the annulment process, here are the typical steps you can expect to take:

- **Step 1:** Meet with your pastor to discuss your situation and confirm your readiness to begin the process. At this point, you may be asked to begin meeting with a parish case assistant — someone who is trained in helping petitioners go through each step of the annulment process. Not all parishes have case assistants, but if you are assigned to one, I believe you will find him or her to be quite helpful. He or she will likely help you gain insight on what grounds seem likely to fit your circumstances. This is a relatively new part of the process (it wasn't being done when I went through mine), but the goal is to help present a more clear-cut case to the tribunal.

- **Step 2:** Select your witnesses and contact them to explain what you are doing and how you would like them to proceed if they agree to be a witness.
- **Step 3:** Fill out the initial paperwork. You may receive the forms to fill out and file from your parish pastor, or in many cases they can be downloaded from the tribunal page on your diocese's website. You will need to provide contact information for your witnesses at this time. Once you send everything in with a copy of your marriage certificate and any other documentation required, it should take anywhere from two weeks to a month to receive a response. If you receive a response sooner than that, you're off to a good start.
- **Step 4:** From there, you will receive the lengthier questionnaire we have discussed, to fill out and return. If you have a case assistant to meet with, don't wait until you meet to begin writing your answers. You can review your answers with the him or her when you meet. (Note: If you have access to an adoration chapel, I highly recommend going there to write your answers so that you can have the consolation and inspiration of the Blessed Sacrament with you as you write.)
- **Step 5:** Once you have returned the questionnaire, you may be scheduled for a personal interview with one of the canon lawyers. Not all dioceses do this, but many do. If so, it will likely be a lengthy interview, so make sure you block off several hours for this.
- **Step 6:** Contact your witnesses to make sure they've completed and returned their paperwork.
- **Step 7:** Wait, pray, and work. Work on the things we discussed in the previous chapter — especially

trusting God and letting this process be a healing one. If the tribunal needs additional information, you will be contacted and asked for it.

The tribunal will collect information regarding the upbringing, dating and engagement, and marriage relationship of both ex-spouses, with particular focus on what happened on the day of the wedding. Through this process, they determine whether or not a valid marriage was brought into being on the day of the wedding.

Here is where we encounter one of the changes Pope Francis initiated within the annulment process: the elimination of a mandatory two-court decision process. Before this change occurred, it was standard that within as little as a few months or as long as a year, both the petitioner and the respondent would receive a *letter in the first instance*. This is a formal declaration of the tribunal's decision, but the case was still required to be reviewed and approved by the local bishop. When that had been done, both the petitioner and the respondent would receive a *letter in the second instance*, which declares the tribunal's decision with full approval. Pope Francis eliminated the requirement for a second approval as a way to reduce the amount of time a petitioner has to wait for a decision. He did not eliminate the *court* of the second instance, which means, if one or the other former spouse wants to appeal the decision, he or she still can. Put simply: A second approval is no longer required. As of the writing of this book, it does not appear that all dioceses have yet adopted this as part of their practice, and some tribunals may still be utilizing the court of the second instance.

If the final letter you and your ex-spouse receive states that no valid marriage was brought into being on the day of the wedding, you are not bound to each other and are free to marry in the Church. This letter is called a *declaration (or decree) of invalidity*, or what is typically referred to as an annulment. If the judges decide that the evidence provided by you, your ex-spouse, and your witnesses does not prove the marriage was invalid, however, they will return a negative decision.

If neither party wishes to appeal, the case is concluded, and the spouses are bound to each other and must honor their marriage vows, even though they may live separately.

It's important to note that there may also be recommendations set forth by the tribunal for further action on the part of the petitioner, such as a mandate that psychological counseling be received *before* one or the other former spouse is permitted to marry again. I have seen this happen many times, and the person receiving the declaration's stipulation must act before being able to marry in the Church again. Nevertheless, this is your final step, unless you decide to appeal the decision.

Understanding the Grounds

Grounds are the specific reasons why a tribunal could decide a marriage is not valid. It is important to read the actual laws explaining the various grounds, and they can be found at the Vatican's website (www.vatican.va). Below, I have provided the specific canons in which each of the grounds can be found. The following brief explanations are only meant to provide a simple understanding of what grounds for your annulment might be sought and are not limited to the particular circumstances described:

- **Lack of Use of Reason (Canon 1095.1):** This canon would be used in a case to provide an argument that a person was suffering from some form of mental illness at the time of consent, which would prohibit that person from making important decisions such as a lifelong, permanent commitment to one person.
- **Lack of Due Discretion (Canon 1095.2):** This canon would be used as grounds to prove that one or the other spouse lacked the maturity to understand the essential matrimonial rights and obligations that must be mutually given and respected between two spouses.

- **Inability to Assume (Canon 1095.3):** This canon is used as grounds in a case where one or the other spouse has an impediment to committing to a lifelong, exclusive union, such as sexual addiction or homosexual tendencies, which prohibit the ability to use proper judgment or discernment regarding matrimonial rights and obligations.
- **Fraud (Canon 1098):** This canon is used to support a case where one or both spouses misrepresented themselves or kept hidden knowledge critical to each other's freedom to consent to be married. For example, if a woman has had an abortion and doesn't disclose this to her fiancé because she knows he won't marry her if she does, so she decides to keep that part of her past a secret, that would be fraud.
- **Error (Canon 1099):** This canon is used in cases where one spouse has misrepresented his or her intentions or capabilities regarding the duties and responsibilities of marriage. An example of this would be if one of the spouses has received permanent contraceptive services such as a vasectomy or tubal ligation but did not inform the other spouse before the wedding.
- **Partial and Total Simulation (Canon 1101):** This canon is used in a case where one or both spouses consent to marriage without believing in the permanency of marriage or intending to create a permanent, lifelong union.
- **Force and Fear (Canon 1103):** This canon is used to support a case where one or both spouses were forced into the marriage or were threatened with negative consequences if the marriage did not take place.

Some Final Thoughts

After reading through these steps and explanations, I hope you've come to a clearer understanding of what the annulment process entails, and that it doesn't seem as daunting as it did before.

However, I can completely understand if you still feel overwhelmed by the idea of writing essay answers about some very painful memories. Maybe you just can't bring yourself to revisit the things that caused you such grief. "Divorce is already such a heavy cross, why would I take this on as well?" you might be thinking. If that is the case, you may need to step back from considering this as an option, at least for the moment, and that's perfectly okay.

But allow me to offer you some food for thought that might help you take this important step. Odd as it sounds, there is a peace that comes from suffering when you know that you're doing it the right way. True, it's hard to see the crosses we bear as something good for us, but it's a fact that these sufferings can be fruitful. They can help us mature in our faith and mature in wisdom. If we let them, our hurts can elevate our ability to love. And in some way, they can bring us peace. "Really?" you're probably thinking. "Peace through suffering?" It sounds insane, I know, and it is completely countercultural, but it's true.

By going through the annulment process, you are seeking a spiritual truth with humility and trusting the action of the Holy Spirit. You can offer up the suffering that comes with revisiting these painful memories for your own good and for the benefit of others, meaning you can attach spiritual and eternal meaning to it. But more importantly, going through the annulment process is a step toward finding forgiveness for your ex-spouse. Forgiveness sets you free and increases your ability to love. As Father Tadeusz Dajczer expresses it so poignantly in his book *The Gift of Faith* (one of my favorites):

> [W]e must open ourselves to Christ and feel like helpless children in the face of the crushing waves of negative feelings. We must have the attitude of a child who is helpless when faced with matters relating to God, people, the surroundings and the environment. This is an attitude of trusting faith, believing that Jesus, Himself, will come and will love in us even those whom we do not like. It is this kind of attitude that will enable us to come to the agape love. Ultimately, when negative feelings increase in

us or at least the positive feelings fade, only Christ is able to love in us. Thanks to Him, our will should have a freedom from emotions, or at least, it should strive to have this kind of freedom.[8]

No matter what you feel, you can make the choice to forgive. I know this can be very difficult to put into practice. Maybe your ex-spouse is a real jerk (and I don't just mean men; women can be real jerks too). Maybe you can barely face your ex-spouse. Maybe you were in an abusive relationship and have sustained terrible hurts over a long period of time. There could be many reasons why it's difficult to revisit these old wounds, and they're probably all justified. But if you think of what Jesus did when he was being nailed to the cross, he asked forgiveness for his enemies: "Father, forgive them; for they know not what they do" (Lk 23:34). This is something the annulment process can bring about: forgiveness for those who have hurt you, and the ability to make peace with the past. The healing that comes from those two things alone is amazing.

QUICK POINTS RECAP

- The annulment questionnaire is very personal in nature because marriage is very personal. The goal of asking probing questions is not to embarrass you or your witnesses, but to gather as much information as possible and make an accurate and informed decision about your case.

- The annulment questionnaire helps you take an objective look at what happened, including all the mistakes and poor choices, and this knowledge becomes instrumental in helping you make better choices in the future.

---

8. Father Tadeusz Dajczer, *The Gift of Faith*, 2nd Edition (In the Arms of Mary Foundation edition, 2001), pp. 212–213.

- The best way to begin the process is to meet with your pastor and discuss your situation. From there, you can begin to familiarize yourself with the grounds, select your witnesses, and fill out the initial paperwork with your case assistant (if you have been assigned one).

- Pope Francis did not eliminate courts of the second instance; he only eliminated the *requirement* for cases to have a second approval. Appeals to decisions may still be made.

- If the final letter you and your former spouse receive states that a valid marriage was not brought into being on the day of your wedding, you are free to marry. This letter is called a declaration (or decree) of invalidity and is what is commonly referred to as an annulment.

QUESTIONS FOR REFLECTION

1. What are the reasons I want to go through the annulment process?

2. Do I understand the necessity of writing, as detailed as possible, an account of what happened for the questionnaire? Why or why not?

3. What am I hoping to get out of the annulment process?

4. How do I think the decision, either way, will change my life?

CHAPTER FIVE

"A Time to Weep, and a Time to Laugh"
Encouragement for When the Going Gets Tough

We've covered a lot of material so far, and maybe you feel ready to roll up your sleeves and jump in, which is great — or maybe you still have some hesitation. Either way, now is the perfect time to talk about something that can happen as people begin the annulment process: they start losing steam at some point and end up dropping the ball. It's not guaranteed to happen, but it does happen to many because, as we discussed before, revisiting all the unpleasant memories can take an emotional toll. Trying to sift through all of the memories can feel like it's too much to bear, or just a painful waste of your time.

Once again, I assure you that good will come out of this exercise if you persevere. Confronting those hard truths head-on, acknowledging and accepting what really happened, and cleansing the wounds allow you to make peace with the past and lay it to rest. It brings a palpable sense of relief. But in the thick of it, you might find yourself overwhelmed by all those memories and hit an emotional brick wall, which is quite normal and understandable.

The goal of this chapter is to offer you some encouragement along the way. Some memories will hurt, but not everything you remember will be sad. You will remember the good times in your marriage relationship as well. For the purposes of this discussion, though, I'll give you some concrete steps to take when the going gets tough so that you can have the appropriate motivation to persevere and complete all the necessary steps of the annulment process. There is a great sense of accomplishment even in that.

Divorce as a Path to Sainthood

When I was about ten years old, back in the early '70s, my mom and dad took my brothers, sisters, and me to a Catholic parish in San Clemente, California, to hear Mother Teresa of Calcutta give a talk. Of course, the auditorium was jammed with people tripping over one another to find even the tiniest space to squeeze into and listen to her speak. My family arrived early, and we were lucky enough to get seats.

As I listened to that tiny woman, dressed in white and blue, speak, my mother leaned over and whispered in my ear, "Never forget this day. You are in the presence of a living saint." That day is preserved in my mind as if it had just happened a few months ago.

My parents said the same thing to me a few years later, on a Sunday afternoon, as we were rushing out the door to attend a Mass that was going to be celebrated by Cardinal József Mindszenty, a Hungarian archbishop who was unjustly punished and imprisoned for his vehement and outspoken stance against Communism. "We *already* went to Mass this morning. Why do we have to go to Mass AGAIN?" I complained. And, as before, the emphasis was placed on the rare opportunity being presented: "Because you will be in the presence of a living saint!"

At my young age, I could tell that this was important — based upon my parents' reactions — but I didn't really appreciate the opportunity I had at the time. Now, as an adult, I'm so grateful to my parents for impressing upon me the importance of striving to be holy and the impact that paying attention to those who are holy, as examples, can have on my own life. I think there are many people alive today who truly are living saints, walking among us, often very much unnoticed. That's just how they are becoming holy, through living the small details of everyday life with great love.

God offers each of us opportunities to become saints according to our state in life, and this, without question, includes the suffering that comes with going through a divorce and any suffering you might encounter in the annulment process. What, exactly, does this look like for someone who is divorced? The annulment process presents opportunities to live the small details of your life with great love, a love that can transform you into a different person — stronger, wiser, and more merciful.

First, revisiting those painful memories of your relationship with your ex-spouse can seem like cruel and unusual punishment, but it is possible to approach this with great love. For example, you could offer up this pain for the good of someone else, maybe even for your ex-spouse, if you've been able to get to a place where you can actually pray for him or her.

Second, you could approach this task of completing the questionnaire with a desire to find forgiveness for those who have hurt you.

Next, you may find it awkward and uncomfortable to ask friends and family to offer witness testimony. It is a humbling position to be in, no question. Yet this is an opportunity for you to continue to live the small details with great love, through your humility and reliance on God, as you work with your witnesses and wait patiently for their replies. Sometimes the patience aspect alone is a great exercise in virtue.

But perhaps the greatest opportunity the annulment process offers for you to grow in holiness is the period of waiting that takes place when you have completed all the necessary requirements on your end. Thus begins a period of silence and patience with the tribunal as it makes its determination. It can seem unbearable to wait for the case to be processed and a verdict rendered. If you're a control freak, as I am, you can drive yourself crazy wondering what will happen. Yet here is an opportunity to show great love every day by using this period of time to work on building your trust in God and finding acceptance for whatever the decision might be.

My friend Chris Easterly shares his perspective on this time of waiting for an answer:

As we exited church after Mass, I ran into the deacon who's guiding me through my annulment process. We shook hands and smiled. "Keep your patience, brother," he said.

It's been about six months since we submitted all the material (questionnaire, forms, witnesses, etc.) to the local marriage tribunal, and now we're just waiting on a decision. I'd love to know what's going on behind the scenes. I'd love to get a decision right away. But, at this point, all I can do is "keep my patience."

As James 1:4 says: "Let endurance have its perfect result so that you may be perfect and complete, lacking in nothing" [NASB]. Easier said than done, of course. But I feel like God has been showing me through this whole process that all I'm called to do is be faithful, take the necessary steps to apply for the annulment, and then … just be patient. Honestly, what else can I do?

During this waiting period, I have a lot of questions. Will the tribunal grant my petition for nullity? Will they determine that my marriage was sacramental after all? If so, how will I accept the decision? And whether my marriage is annulled or not, what will life look like moving forward after all this?

I've found that the best way to deal with all these questions and emotions is to try to simply leave them in God's hands. After all, what good does it do to constantly think about and obsess over the eventual result? As Jesus said, "Which of you by worrying can add a single hour to his life's span?" (Luke 12:25 [NASB]).

So for now, what I say to others waiting on a decision is what my deacon told me. Keep the patience, brother. Be patient, sister. Trust that God is at work, even when you can't see it or feel it. And trust that the God who is at work behind the scenes is a God who loves you and wants the best for you.

You are not alone in your desire to have answers. There are many others out there, like Chris, who understand what you have to endure. Most importantly, God knows. He sees everything, he knows your heart, and he knows how to give you a future that will make you happy.

When I was at this point in the annulment process, there were times I would be so distracted by my worries over what the decision would be that I wasn't really present in my own life! I was placing myself in a future that hadn't happened yet, and I found myself constantly stressed out over something that was completely out of my control. So, to preserve my sanity (and believe me, I am a super control-freak, like over-the-top, so giving up control in this manner was difficult for me), I created a little mantra for myself, a simple prayer I could immediately pray when I felt my worries, over what might happen, taking over. I simply said, "I will be happy with whatever you give me, Lord." I knew quite well that there were no guarantees I would receive a decree of invalidity, so the only way I could live peacefully with myself was to trust God — trust him to inspire the canon lawyers with a truthful decision, and trust that no matter which way the pendulum swung, his plan for my life would be happy and fulfilling. It was like standing at the edge of a cliff, closing my eyes, and jumping off, trusting that God would catch me.

He did.

So fear not, and make this your special project. Don't drive yourself crazy wondering what will happen. Just tell God you trust him. If you don't really feel it, ask him to help you trust him more. Do this often. Pray for the canon lawyers reviewing your case, and wait with patience. It can be scary, but the only thing that will really, ultimately, make us happy is to have God's will be done in our life.

I know that doesn't sound like the way people do things these days. We're always so full of demands and extremely impatient when we have to wait. But therein lies the essence of living the small details with great love: just put your faith in God, and trust that the outcome will be what he wants for your life. And you can absolutely trust that *that* is what will make you happy.

Not only are these little ways to live the details with great love, but they also are steps that lead down the path to holiness. These are the steps that all the saints took, famous or not. They endured their crosses with humility, forgiveness, and patience.

What to Do When You Hit the Emotional Brick Wall

Accomplishing any goal or preparing for any sort of difficulty requires a plan and some tools. This is especially true when it comes to planning how you will persevere when you hit the emotional brick wall while going through the annulment process. Your plan going in should be to live the small details with great love, no matter how tempting it is to react differently. From there, identify the tools that will help you accomplish this.

Here are some tools you can pick up and use immediately.

1. Go to Confession as Often as You Can

No matter if you go to confession once a month or haven't confessed in years, I encourage you to start going more frequently, especially when you are overwhelmed by emotions. Why? Because as you go through this process, the emotions you experience will bring up anger and resentment, and there is no better place to resolve these feelings than in the confessional. You receive many great graces there, graces that help you persevere, graces that make it possible to forgive. Try to find a priest who can provide good counsel that will give you something to reflect upon.

This sacrament is a fantastic tool to keep at hand. If you haven't been to confession in many years, now is the time to encounter it again.

2. Create Your Own Mantra

You'll really need this when life gets overwhelming, especially if the emotions start to spill out in a place where you can't really be alone with your feelings. "Jesus, I trust in you!" — which conveys your desire to let God take over — is a great little prayer to say when emotions or worries start to get out of control. Create something to say or pray that will be like a reset button. It can help you to refocus on the fact that this part of the process is out of your control and in God's hands, and that you will trust him with it.

3. *Journal Your Way to a Peaceful Heart*

One of the most powerful ways to get yourself through a tough time is to write in a journal, daily — or as often as you can. There is something therapeutic about getting those thoughts and concerns out of your heart, out of your head, and onto a piece of paper. From there, you can burn it, share it with a trusted confidant, or bring it to Eucharistic Adoration to pray about it. Probably the most powerful thing about your journal will be picking it up years later and seeing just how far God has brought you. I've done this myself, and it is an amazing thing to look back and see all of God's mercy, all of his grace at work in my life.

4. *Pray the Rosary and the Divine Mercy Chaplet*

Both of these prayers are extremely powerful in bringing about the peace and trust we need during this period of time. They aren't good-luck charms or quick-fix solutions, so we shouldn't be superstitious when we pray them or look for sudden changes that aren't realistic. But they can be powerful channels of grace and peace.

Sandy McKay, a wonderful Catholic therapist in the Atlanta area, tells her clients all the time to pray the Rosary for healing, but she emphasizes that it's important not to look for feelings or big changes when we do. She says, "I've had many clients say to me, 'I've been praying my Rosary every day for years, and that hasn't changed my ex one bit!' And I tell them, 'Well, it looks like the wrong person got changed!' "

The changes we should look for are the ones that will take place within ourselves, and then leave it to God to work in the hearts of others.

5. *Use This Unique Period of Time in Your Life Wisely, Because You'll Never Have It Again*

Wow, that almost sounds romantic, doesn't it? Well, my point is not to romanticize it but to emphasize the importance of the gift of this time. Now is the time to reflect on the knowledge you have acquired and how you will allow that to shape your future decisions. Maybe there are behaviors in yourself that you have recognized in revisiting your dating, engagement, and married life — behaviors that you want to change. Now is the time to work on those things. All of this will not only keep you focused on good things, but it will also help prepare you for whatever decision will be handed down.

Also, laugh and be grateful. These are two very important tools in rebuilding your life after divorce. Once you have completed your part in the annulment process and all you have left to do is wait for a verdict, you need to focus on lighter things. Now is the perfect opportunity to find the beauty in life and cultivate your sense of humor again. This doesn't necessarily mean being "funny," but trying to live life with more levity. Learn to laugh at yourself (again or for the first time), and try not to be too serious. Spend time with friends who can help you live cheerfully. Embracing humor leads to a spirit of gratitude, something all divorced people need in their lives, especially when good things come about as a result of the divorce.

Yes, people don't often see blessings as a result of divorce, but they do happen. In my own experience, I had a difficult time finding things to be grateful for after my divorce, but I knew I wouldn't really move forward in the healing process if I didn't at least try to cultivate a spirit of gratitude. So I began with the little things — you know, the things that everyone should acknowledge and be grateful for, like breathing. Each day I woke up and could breathe, and I was grateful. I just went from there. I was healthy, I lived in a free country, I had a good job, and so on. This new habit of finding things to be grateful for also made it easier for me to pray. Now I had something to pray about! But the biggest impact it had on me was the day I realized that something very good had happened as a result of my divorce.

During the time we were married, my ex-spouse had constantly taunted and made fun of me for practicing my faith. Yes, I did marry a Catholic, but he pretty much dropped out of the Faith right after we got married. He always belittled me for attending Mass and going to confession, and he tried to make me feel like a loser. After a while, I realized I was now free to live my Catholic faith fully! It was a tremendous blessing. Is there anything in your life you can be grateful for that has been a direct result of your divorce?

Finally, I can't encourage you enough to remember that your divorce does not define you: it's only something that happened to you. God created you with a distinct purpose in life, and a civil-divorce decree does not change that. As I had mentioned at the beginning of this book, divorce is devastating — and, yes, it hurts so bad that it feels as though it should have killed you ... but it didn't. You're still alive, and you have more life to live. Being in possession of that piece of paper doesn't take away your purpose in life. It doesn't negate all the gifts and talents God gave you from the very beginning. It doesn't cancel out all the good things you've done or have yet to do. It's an event that took place in your life, and God wants you to heal from it so that you can continue fulfilling your purpose.

QUICK POINTS RECAP

- The annulment process can bear great spiritual and emotional fruit in your life as you accept and acknowledge the truth of what happened in your relationship.

- The annulment process is a great way to live the small details with great love through offering up your suffering for your own good and the good of others.

- Receiving the Sacrament of Reconciliation, creating a mantra to pray when things get overwhelming, journaling, praying the Rosary and Divine Mercy Chaplet, and finding a spirit of levity and gratitude are all helpful tools when the going gets tough during this process.

- Blessings likely have come about as a result of your divorce, and this is the time to discover and acknowledge them.

QUESTIONS FOR REFLECTION

1. In reflecting upon all that happened in my relationship with my former spouse, is there any memory I am afraid or reluctant to recall for the purposes of answering the questionnaire? If so, why?

2. Are there people in my life who could benefit from my offering up the task of answering the annulment process? Who are those people?

3. Is there anything in my life that has happened as a direct result of my divorce that I can be grateful for? What are those things?

CHAPTER SIX

"A Time to Keep Silence, and a Time to Speak"
How Friends and Family Can Help

One of the aspects of being divorced and Catholic I find particularly heartbreaking is the disconnect that is created when loved ones and friends of someone who gets divorced have no understanding of how to support him or her. Have you ever had someone say something to you in response to your situation that angered you or made you even more depressed? Something like, "It's been nine months now, you need to start getting over it already" or "Don't worry, we'll find you someone new." These statements are mostly innocent, springing out of an awkwardness over your situation, which I will go into further in a moment. But the real handicap of the situation is that most Catholics who have not been divorced don't really understand how to connect with or show compassion to someone who is struggling because of divorce, and they feel awkward and frustrated about it. This is why I'm hoping you will share this chapter with anyone you are close to that can benefit from help in this area. For the next several pages, I will be speaking primarily to them.

A Family Affair

There is no question that the most valued and appreciated gift someone who is divorced can receive is a family member or friend who reaches out with genuine concern. I have heard countless stories of men and women who say there was one person in particular who made a difference for them after their divorce. These people made it possible for them to hang on through those dark days and cling to hope when they felt there was none.

The presence of someone who cares means the world to someone suffering this way, even if he doesn't say it openly, or even if she is too distraught to thank you for being there. That caring presence means the world to them. Frequently, however, people want to help but don't actually know how. The suggestion makes them feel awkward, or they feel they don't have the right words to say when it comes right down to it. The most important thing you can offer your loved ones going through divorce is your presence in their lives.

Divorced men and women are often lumped into the same category as widows and widowers, since both groups have lost their spouses. It makes sense to equate divorce with the death of a spouse, but while there are some similarities, there are also stark differences. Losing a spouse through death is a different kind of pain than losing your spouse in divorce. A widow or widower grieves the loss of a spouse who can never return. And while every marriage has issues, they often grieve the loss of a strong and healthy love relationship, which is devastating.

On the other hand, someone who is divorced grieves the loss of a spouse who has not died and is still present in their lives in many ways. The absent spouse has deliberately rejected the requirement of living together as husband and wife and maintaining an intact family. The ex-spouse often continues to hurt and antagonize, causing grave discord with children, in-laws, and extended family. It's difficult to heal from wounds that are constantly re-opened.

When someone is widowed, caring relatives and friends usually descend upon them with flowers, meals, visits, etc., showering them with attention and compassion. Don't get me wrong, this is very good, and it should happen. But divorced people rarely, if ever, receive this sort of treatment as they set about trying to pick up the pieces.

A divorced person has to deal with rejection on many, many levels: the rejection of the spouse who leaves; oftentimes, the rejection of neighbors and friends who feel too awkward to continue the friendship; the rejection of the in-laws; and the rejection of their own children (a very unfortunate, yet very common, occurrence). The losses that follow compound this feeling of rejection: losing a home or other possessions; losing parental rights over children; losing human touch on a daily basis (no hugs to wake up to or goodnight kisses); losing your marital status, and so forth.

Definitely one of the most difficult aspects of dealing with divorce is that in the face of all this personal devastation, life still goes on. Bills still have to be paid. Kids still have to go to school. Responsibilities still have to be taken care of. And the divorced person is expected to put on a smile and keep going as if nothing has happened. So it makes sense, then, that having the companionship of someone who truly cares, takes a personal interest, and takes time out of his or her day to check in and see if everything is all right is so very important and meaningful.

A great example of someone who needed a caring person like this when he was going through his divorce is my friend Bill. Bill wanted to remain married to his wife and work out their differences, but she was adamant about splitting up. Bill always said that until the very last moment, as he was moving his things out of his house, he was hoping and praying his soon-to-be ex-wife would change her mind and reconcile. Nevertheless, he ended up moving into a tiny apartment while she and their two boys stayed in the family home. The judge ruled that he could have visitation with his boys every other weekend. On those designated Fridays, he would pick them up, spend the best weekend with them he could provide, and return them home to their mom Sunday evening.

The two things that kept him going during that terribly depressing time were going to Eucharistic Adoration after he dropped off his boys (because Jesus' presence in the monstrance saved him from his devastating sorrow) and, surprisingly enough, holding hands during the Our Father with other congregants during Sunday Mass. The connection he said he felt during Mass made him feel that he was part of a community, connected to a family. Those few moments of hand-holding were often the only physical contact he had in the two weeks between visits with his sons. Imagine that.

Divorce is a terribly lonely and alienating experience, and people who go through it need to be reminded that they're still an important part of their families and their communities. This is why your presence in their lives matters to them so much. But often, people shy away from making themselves available, and this happens for many reasons. Sometimes, it's because divorce is such a controversial subject in the Church. People don't like to talk about it because they don't understand how to reconcile the fact that someone they care about is in a situation the Church directly teaches we should not be in. *Are they sinning? Are they innocent victims?* It can be hard to tell, and this makes people uncomfortable and unwilling to get involved.

Sometimes, unfortunately, other Catholics who are not divorced deliberately avoid those who are, often with an air of disdain. A few years ago, I received this email from a woman, who asked to remain anonymous, describing her experience:

Dear Lisa,

I am a Catholic who was divorced by my husband three years ago when I became seriously ill. We had been married nearly thirty years. I lost all our mutual friends, including those who were Catholic. He transferred to another parish, but I stayed in the parish we had been members of for over fifteen years, thinking of it as my home. It turned out to be quite the opposite.

Unfortunately, none of my Catholic friends reached out to me, and in my home diocese there was and still is nothing in the way of emotional, psychological, or spiritual support for someone going through a divorce. I finally turned to a local Methodist church that offered support groups for people recovering from divorce.

Although I'd served as a Eucharistic minister taking Communion to the home-bound, served as a lector, participated in Bible study, and sponsored two people who had come into the Church, as well as attending daily Mass frequently and weekly Adoration on Friday evenings for many years, after my divorce I was suddenly invisible —

erased, as it were. I was so isolated, I even experienced several cycles of suicidal loneliness despite my attempts to find new friendships in various diocesan groups. The indifference I faced left me bitter, and I finally left the parish for another to escape the temptations to anger and resentment.

In effect, I was not loved but shunned.

It is now a little over three years since the divorce, and I am much healthier and happier, but not because my fellow Catholics cared. I believe I made it through because of my devotion to Our Lady and a prayer life of many years.

I am still a practicing Catholic. As Peter said to the Lord, "Where else shall we go? You have the words of everlasting life." But I do understand why Catholics facing this kind of indifference leave the Church. I am inclined to think that my experience of abandonment is far more the norm in the Church in this country than not.

I think many Catholics look upon those who are divorced as sinners, and those divorced single parents with children often find themselves in the cold because former friends fear their children will somehow be contaminated by associating with children from a broken family.

I speculate that these kinds of attitudes may be behind the consternation many Catholics feel about Pope Francis reaching out to divorced, and even to remarried Catholics.

But given that nearly 25 percent of American Catholics are divorced, it is pastorally irresponsible to not reach out to those who find themselves in that situation for many reasons.

Perhaps if the Church had better outreach in the first place, many Catholics would not have left and remarried outside the Church. (And this is leaving aside the problems caused by lack of proper catechesis and marriage preparation.)

I was heartbroken to read this email, but I've heard similar stories over the years. This woman's story illustrates why, as often as possible, I try to tell Catholics who have never experienced divorce that reaching out to someone going through this terrible event does not mean you condone divorce. It simply means you are willing to help that person carry his or her cross through your generous attention. We must remember the words of Pope Francis, when he said we should all be going out to the battlefield to find the wounded and bring them back to the field hospital that is the Church.

There are some excellent ways you can do this, and there are also some things you should avoid. Below are some helpful tips for helping your loved one through this difficult time.

Choose Your Words Carefully

"You're better off without him, Lisa! Don't worry, there's someone better out there for you."

Those words kept ringing in my ears as I drove home that Thanksgiving evening, back in 1993. I was overwhelmed by anger, sadness, and bewilderment as I struggled to understand why this relative of mine, Dave, thought it was a good idea to say that to me.

We were at my parents' home for the holiday feast, and being the only divorced member of my big, fat, Catholic family, there was definitely a sense of awkwardness when it came to conversation. In an attempt to say something positive, Dave uttered those stinging words. I bit my tongue for fear of saying something I would regret and just walked away with my broken heart in pieces again.

"I don't want someone new; I want my husband back!" I shouted, without speaking a word. *Why in the world would he say such a thing?* I knew he was just trying to be nice about it, but those words hurt.

Attending family gatherings when you're divorced can be quite difficult, because the focus on coming together with friends and relatives definitely has a way of amplifying the loss of your own marriage and intact family. Unfortunately, there always seems to be plenty of awkward "advice" that is dispensed by well-meaning family members.

Over the years, I probably heard every well-intended remark a person could think of — but in all honesty, they just made me feel worse:

- "Don't worry, we'll find you someone new!"
- "Remember, everything happens for a reason."
- "It's been six months now; it's time to move on!"
- "Stop crying and go find someone who will treat you like the princess you are!"
- "You'll be okay; God has a plan!"

After witnessing the way people tend to react to someone who is going through a divorce, I've come to understand the root of all that graceless advice. People are uncomfortable when they observe someone they know suffering or struggling through a difficult situation. Naturally, they want to do something to help, something to fix it, but they are likely at a loss as to how they can do this. This is often when these well-intended but insensitive statements might slip out. And they hurt. A lot.

So how can you help? What things should you say or do to bring comfort to those who are really struggling with their divorce? Here are my best suggestions for you on this:

- **Don't say anything; just listen and offer a hug instead of words.** It's not necessary to have pearls of wisdom. The best way I can underscore this is in telling you how I felt at this point: I knew in my heart of hearts that the only one who could really help me was my husband. He was the only one who could make my situation right again, but he was gone, never to return. What I needed was someone to listen to me and allow me to talk about the terrible things that had happened to me without making me feel like a complete and total loser. I needed someone who understood that divorce was wrong but didn't judge me for being in this position, a position I was forced into against my will. Luckily for me, I did have a few people like this in my life, and it's true — their presence and concern were a great blessing to me.
- **Say things like, "I'm here for you, if you need me."** Then, really be there when they need you. This might

mean they'll show up on your doorstep out of the blue one day, or possibly you'll receive a desperate call at 2 a.m. (I've had to make a few of those), and it might be inconvenient or even irritating for you. But for the suffering person to know that when things seem overwhelming or hopeless, there is an anchor somewhere — someone who wants to help — that means the world to him or her.

- **Check in every few days or so to see how they're doing.** Another friend of mine, Liz, was absolutely crushed when her husband walked out one evening. Her three young children were devastated by the way this happened, and Liz was determined to keep a brave face when her children were with her, always reminding them to pray for Daddy. She took time to grieve when no one would notice, like when the washer and dryer were running and she could go into the laundry room and cry, where no one could hear her. Because she shared this with me, I knew she would need someone touching base with her, and I did. Every couple of days or so, I called her, just to make sure she was okay — well, as okay as could possibly be expected.

- **Offer to take the kids so that they can have some alone time.** Liz chose not to share her emotions with her children, so she really needed some "me" time. In other cases, the ex-spouses need to meet to discuss things (and the kids can't be there), or maybe he has to appear in court, or she needs to go to counseling. There could be many reasons why a divorced person needs this personal time, so don't underestimate the value of just keeping the kids for a few hours. It is an amazing help.

- **Offer to bring a meal.** This, too, is a tremendous help. With divorce, the emotions that one experiences are powerful, and learning how to manage them takes some practice. Suffice it to say, there will be some days when your loved one going through a divorce won't want to get out of bed, will call in sick to work, and may even negate all sense of responsibility. Please don't let this alarm you; it's a normal reaction to what they are going through and also a sign that they need help. Don't be shy about offering to bring a meal, go grocery shopping, or do anything else that needs attention.

- **Invite them to come along with you to Mass, confession, shopping, a day trip, etc.** Even if all you get is a lot of hemming and hawing, know that your reaching out and asking them to be with you still means a lot to them.

- **Encourage them to keep coming to church.** Divorce can make a person feel unwanted, unlovable, unforgiven, and ashamed. It's important for them to know they are still loved by God and have value. This is not because we are trying to overlook or play down the scandal of divorce or the sin of whichever spouse abandoned the family for selfish reasons. You need a starting point, and it's the same starting point God gives us: when you get knocked down, whether it was your fault or not, he is there to love you and help you get back up, not wallow in misery and victimhood. He wants us to get up, brush ourselves off, and get to the business of forgiving — if that's what we have to do — or repenting. It's the same for divorced Catholics. They need to know they are welcome at church.

- **Encourage them not to lower their standards.** This one aspect is, in my opinion, why we have such a crisis in the Church with divorced and civilly remarried Catholics. Divorce is the ultimate discourager and often causes a crisis of faith. This sets the stage for lowering one's standards. The pain and disappointment are so harsh, it's easy to adopt an attitude of "I just don't care," which can be dangerous in many ways. That attitude is what drives many people away from the Church, believing the standards are just too high and unrealistic. Remind your loved one that divorce is not the end of the road, and there will come a day when they will be happy again, even if they don't believe it, and even if it takes a long time. God still has good things in store, he still has a purpose for them to fulfill. These are not platitudes; They are truths that are good to reinforce.

- **Pray for them.** There is no priority to these suggestions, but this, in my opinion, is the best and most effective thing you can do for someone who is going through a divorce. Pray for them, as you see fit — but I highly encourage the Rosary and the Divine Mercy Chaplet. The type of prayers you decide you can pray is not all-important, though; the important thing is that you pray.

- **Keep their business private.** Don't share with others what your divorced loved one has shared with you. Your discretion builds a base of trust and security — security that is harshly violated when a divorce occurs.

- **Be patient with their displays of emotion, fits of tears, or harsh words.** The emotions that come with divorce can be just like a gang of rowdy teenagers who rush in and destroy a room. Unless you played a role in the demise of the marriage, you can be sure you are not the cause of any of those emotions. He or she just hasn't learned to control them yet. In time, that will happen.

- **Remind them how important they are to you and to others.** Affirm their self-worth.

- **Don't encourage them to date or try to fix them up with someone.** As explained in the earlier chapters of this book, dating is not a good idea, especially when being used as a Band-Aid for the pain or as a means to pump up one's self-esteem.

I hope you find these suggestions helpful as you contemplate how you might support someone going through a divorce. But those are my words. Now I'd like to show you real-life examples of what I'm talking about. Here are some stories I've gathered, from other people I know, about how they were helped by considerate, thoughtful, and generous folks during this most miserable period of their lives:

> *Just after my husband decided to end our thirty-year marriage, an acquaintance from my parish saw me crying on the way to my car after Mass. She insisted on meeting me for coffee the next day and brought a bag of materials for me, including a DVD on the life of Saint Rita. More importantly, she told me that after I was finished feeling sorry for myself, not that she blamed me for that, I should remember that marriage is not our destiny — heaven is, and I could focus on that regardless of what happened to my marriage. Jan was the angel I needed, and that day was the beginning of my healing.*
>
> *— Donna*

> *Here are two simple ones that highlight how little kindnesses can mean so much. First, this was soon after my divorce, when I was so overwhelmed with taking care of the house and yard alone. My neighbor, a builder, had someone at his house taking down trees. He walked over and showed me three dead pine trees and had his guys remove them for me. I was so grateful. Second, on my first Mother's Day alone without my children, a friend showed up at my house, with a plant, to wish me Happy Mother's Day. She will never know how much I needed that, and how much that meant to me.*
>
> *— Maria*

> *When I was trying to get my life back together after my divorce, my mom took me on a Catholic Answers cruise, and paid for it! It changed my life and brought me back to the Catholic Church. I experienced great healing by coming back home*

*to the Church, and now I'm giving back by helping others
recover from divorce and return back home to the Church.*

— Paige

*I was in my early thirties, estranged from my family, and
had just gotten out of a very hellish marriage with a raging,
psychotic alcoholic. I was hiding for my life in a hotel room
after fleeing in the middle of the night. I had nothing —
no money, no clothes (she threw everything I had away). I
didn't have a car and had just started a job waiting tables
the week before. I was completely overwhelmed and broken.
My buddy Steve showed up with some money and food and
paid for two days at the hotel for me. I'll never forget that.
It truly saved me.*

— Michael

*I didn't know it at the time of my divorce, but I found out
later that a neighbor I didn't know well was praying fervently
for me through it all. This thought helps me every time I'm
down, and I know it helped then too. I have tried to live up
to her example ever since.*

— Karen

*After going through a very bitter divorce, I was diagnosed
with cancer. Not wanting to draw any attention or pity to my
diagnosis, I shared my surgery date only with close friends.
Thinking I'd be up on my feet within a week or two, I quickly
realized this was going to take a while to recover from. Got
home from the hospital and an army of ladies arrived each
day, for weeks, with vacuums, laundry detergent, and food,
to take care of my, and my kids', needs. What a Godsend!
And an awakening for me that I can and should trust people
to care for me.*

— Ann

The Bottom Line

If we are faithful to the teachings of Christ, we will care for one another, regardless of our hang-ups and differences. Just as the Good Samaritan crossed over to the other side of the road to care for the bloody, beaten man whom everyone else ignored, being there for someone going through a divorce is so important. Caring for one another, nursing hurts, binding wounds — it's all what Jesus does for us. I commend you for taking an interest in helping someone else heal, and I hope you will count on my prayers going forward.

QUICK POINTS RECAP

- Losing a spouse through death is a different kind of pain than losing your spouse in divorce.

- Divorce is a terribly lonely and alienating experience, and people who go through it need to be reminded that they're still an important part of their families and their communities.

- You can help in the following ways:

  › Don't say anything. Just listen and offer a hug instead of words.

  › Say things like, "I'm here for you, if you need me."

  › Check in every few days or so to see how they're doing.

  › Offer to take the kids so that he or she can have some alone time.

  › Offer to bring a meal.

  › Invite them to come along with you to Mass, confession, shopping, for a day trip, etc.

  › Encourage them to keep coming to church.

  › Encourage them not to lower their standards.

  › Pray for them.

> Keep their business private.

> Be patient with their displays of emotion, fits of tears, or harsh words.

> Remind them how important they are to you and to others.

> Don't encourage them to date or try to fix them up with someone.

- If we are faithful to the teachings of Christ, we will care for one another, regardless of our hang-ups and differences.

QUESTIONS FOR REFLECTION

1. Based on the information in this chapter, what is the best way I could help the divorced friend or loved one in my life?

2. If I could place myself in the shoes of someone who is divorced, what kind of things would be important for me to encounter, or ways to be treated, regarding my relationship with others, close to me or not?

"A Time to Mourn, and a Time to Dance"
Healing and Beginning Again

All right. At this point, you've heard a lot of stories from me — and others — and you have digested a lot of information about the annulment process. Now it's time to focus on *you*. Where do you go from here?

Everyone who goes through a divorce, at some point, has to leave the past behind and move forward. And so, your primary goal now should be finding your new direction in life. I think the first reasonable step to take is to decide if going through the annulment process is right for you. So let's take a look at the most common post-divorce scenarios, and how the annulment process would fit into them, to see if this helps you decide what your next step will be.

Common Scenarios That Would Indicate Initiating or Declining the Annulment Process

First Scenario

You may be someone who was married for thirty or forty years or longer, who raised a family, and may now be a grandparent. Suddenly, you find yourself divorced. You might feel that at some point in the future you would like to be in a relationship again, but it's quite common that many people in this situation are not interested in another relationship because they have invested their whole lives in their marriages. If you are not interested in a future relationship and are content to continue as a single person, fulfilling your important role as a parent/grandparent, you are by no means under any obligation to go through the annulment process.

Second Scenario

Maybe you were the one who left your marriage and filed for divorce because of an abusive situation. Alcoholism, drug or pornography addiction, abuse stemming from personality and mental disorders, and physical, sexual, or emotional abuse are all serious problems that plague families in our society today. If it became dangerous for you/your children to remain living with your ex-spouse — especially if he or she was unwilling to change or seek help — a legal separation is permitted by requesting permission from the local bishop. That being said, most people do not know they need permission from their bishop to separate, and you may have gone straight to filing for divorce as a means of starting the process of legal protection.

After such a harrowing experience, it is understandable if you would not be interested in getting remarried. But, overall, it is my experience that the majority of people in this situation do want a future relationship. If you fall into this category, I definitely recommend that you go through the annulment process. Not only can it help you to know if you are free to remarry, but it can also bring much healing from the past and assistance in guiding your choice of spouse in the future.

Third Scenario

Maybe you were abandoned by your spouse and forced into a divorce because of the no-fault divorce laws in your state. This is the situation for many divorced Catholics. Because of this, you might decide you will remain faithful to your vows as a married person, continue raising your children, and live as a single person in society. If you choose to do this, there is no need to initiate the annulment process.

However, you may decide to go through the annulment process, not just because you want to know if you are free to remarry but also to know if you truly had a valid union or not. Knowing that one detail can be quite helpful in sorting out the details of the loss of your marriage and helping you move forward.

You might find out that you never had a valid union and are free to remarry in the Church. You might also discover that you actually do have a valid marriage, even though you are divorced. You may choose, then, to live as a single person from that point forward. In a situation such as this, many people (including me) have investigated the religious life, to see if that is a lifestyle to which they are being called. But another possible outcome of finding out your marriage was indeed valid is that it provides you with the opportunity to reconcile with your ex-spouse, if that is possible. Many couples have reconciled and reunited after divorce, so it is possible.

Fourth Scenario
Maybe you have been divorced and civilly remarried and want to come back to full communion in the Church. You should most definitely begin the annulment process if you are in this situation. You may find that you did not have a valid marriage with your former spouse and can then have your current marriage convalidated in the Church, which would be a very joyful event. If, however, you find you did have a valid marriage with your former spouse, you would then need to consider whether to separate from your current spouse (which is not recommended if you have children) or remain living together as a family, but only as brother and sister with your spouse.

———————————

These are the most common scenarios people who are divorced face these days and, hopefully, taking a look at these situations will help you decide which step you will take next.

But what if you still aren't emotionally ready to take the leap and initiate the process? No worries. Don't put too much pressure on yourself to do this if you feel it is too much for you at this point. It will always be there for you. Just one word of caution: If you think in the future you will want to do this, it is best not to wait *too* long. If you allow a significant period of time to pass between your divorce and starting the annulment process, you will have a difficult time dredging up all the painful memories and details you have tried so hard to forget, and getting witnesses will be more difficult. A good rule of thumb is to start the annulment process one to two years after your divorce, but not much longer than two years. If you've already remarried, it would be a good idea to discuss this with your spouse to make sure he or she understands that it will be an emotionally heavy experience, and be confident that you have his or her support in going through it.

Making the Most of This Time

In the end, if you decide you would like to go through the annulment process, I recommend taking the following steps to make this time in your life as positive and fruitful as possible.

1. Transform from Being Emotionally Crippled to Emotionally Strong

In the first few years after my divorce, and then some, I cried many tears and suffered emotionally for a very long time. But one day it hit me like a bolt of lightning just how much I hated being in that emotional rut. A more important realization was that I was the one — the only one — who could change that. Pity parties were a frequent event on the weekends, and sadness seemed to permeate everything I did. It was that moment I mentioned at the beginning of this book: I suddenly became *sick and tired of being sick and tired*. I wasn't quite sure how to move forward, but I had definitely come to the decision that I was ready to try. I didn't like feeling stuck where I was, and I knew there had to be more to life than this terrible stage of grief I had been going through.

I thought hard about my situation and felt confident that, despite my divorce, I was still called to be married. I had felt that way my whole life, and failing at it the first time didn't change that for me. However, at that point, I was not ready in any way to begin a new relationship, so the obvious step would be to prepare myself for one in the future. I knew that going through the annulment process was a huge part of that step, so I got the ball rolling, with the hopes of getting through it and laying that chapter of my life to rest.

I also decided I was going to work on myself to change any bad habits or negative behavior patterns I had developed and, more importantly, change my perspective on life. I didn't want to see the future as just some big dead end; I wanted to have positive, new experiences, and the only one who could make that happen was me. I had to start doing it on my own, which I did, and I found many new and wonderful experiences. This also helped me to have a much more positive attitude when it came to rolling up my sleeves and doing my share of the work in the annulment process. So, as you begin your own journey through the annulment process, I recommend starting with this same step.

2. Lay Your Cards on the Table
It helps to plan ahead before you start that initial paperwork. Lay all your cards on the table. For example, think about when you will have a block of time to write your answers to the questionnaire. Do you work two jobs or very long hours? You may need to take a few weekends in a row, by yourself, to start answering questions. You may need to get a babysitter to stay with the kids so that you can go to a different location and can focus on your writing.

Also, who will your witnesses be? Witnesses need to be people who had regular contact with you and your ex-spouse during your marriage. It's a good idea to make a list of people who fall into this category before you start asking anyone to fill this role, in case someone can't or doesn't want to.

Another big consideration is how you will spend your time during the waiting period. During the paperwork stage, working on the questionnaire, submitting documents, and keeping your witnesses on track help to give you a feeling of having some control — which is good. But when it's all done, and all you have is time to wait on a decision, it can be hard.

I remember this period in my life quite well. If you're a control freak like I am, the "what if?" scenarios that keep playing out in your head can start to mess with you. In my case, they even made me a little crazy. So the first thing I did was make peace with the unknown. I refused to be afraid of whatever the decision was going to be, and to help me with this I used the mantra I mentioned earlier: "I will be happy with whatever you give me, Lord." That worked well. Whenever those "what if's" started getting me worried, I just said that mantra a few times under my breath — sometimes aloud, if I was alone — and put it all in God's hands. This brought me a lot of peace.

I also stayed busy. Instead of pity parties on the weekend, I went to the driving range at the golf course and worked on my swing. I went to a park and read that book I'd been wanting to read but never had time for. I picked blueberries and canned some jam. I took a trip into Manhattan and spent the day at the Metropolitan Museum of Art, and so on. I wasn't super comfortable doing things by myself, but in the end it was an exercise that did me mountains of good and kept me focused on the right things.

Most of all, I worked on my spiritual life, which had suffered tremendously since my divorce. It was in doing this that my self-esteem was restored. I realized, even though I had felt I was wearing a huge scarlet "D" for so long and that everyone knew I was a failure, that was not how God saw me. Through prayer, reflection, and frequenting the sacraments, God's love for me became a clear and constant joy in my life. He transformed the darkness I had been carrying with me into light, and I became a completely new person.

3. Work on Your Relationship with God

It's so easy after going through a divorce to feel as if God is ignoring you, or that he doesn't care what happens to you. Some people's faith in God and his love for them are never shaken during such a terrible trial, but oftentimes your reaction can be one of complete bewilderment and cause you to feel abandoned, even by God. If you find yourself in this situation, I would like to share one last story with you to illustrate my final point.

Back in January 2002, I was at a conference for the Catholic Radio Association in Miami, Florida. This was just four months after the devastating terror attacks of September 11, 2001. One of the guest speakers — I don't remember his name — was a survivor of the attack on the World Trade Center. Several of his relatives were firefighters who lost their lives that day. And as he stood at the podium in front of hundreds of people and recounted his very tragic and emotional story, he said something I will never forget: "On September 11th, all Americans became New Yorkers, and all the rest of the world became Americans."

I'm sure you yourself can attest to the fact that on that day the whole world was standing with us in our shock and horror. The whole world cried with us. The whole world was filled with compassion for the victims of that attack and showed their solidarity in whatever way they could: candlelight vigils, memorials, waving American flags, etc.

We've seen this sort of compassionate, unified attitude happen on a global scale since that day with other tragedies that have taken place. For example, "*Je suis Charlie*" became a popular phrase after the *Charlie Hebdo* shootings, in France (January 7, 2015). It means "I am Charlie," which conveys the sentiment "I stand with you; I'm with you."

As a divorced Catholic, you may feel as if you are going through your own personal September 11th. There is total devastation on so many levels. But you don't have the whole world uniting in compassion for your suffering. In fact, many people shy away and leave you alone. Add to that the feeling of being ignored by God, and things can seem beyond depressing and discouraging.

But God is with you. That may sound like a platitude, but it's surely not — and if you'd like to see some proof that God truly is with you during this terrible time, just meditate on the mysteries of the Rosary. The Rosary is full of moments in Christ's life in which you can directly see his love for you.

In contemplating Jesus' life as we do in the mysteries of the Rosary, we can hear God saying to us, "I am with you." The almighty Creator of the universe didn't have to come down from heaven and become one of us, but he did — that's him saying, "I am with you." When he was baptized in the Jordan River, he wasn't getting baptized because he needed to be cleansed of sin, because he was sinless. When he stood there and let John the Baptist pour the water over him, he was showing us, "I am with you." When he wrestled with doing God's will and not his own in the Garden of Gethsemane the night before he died and took on the sins of all mankind, that was him showing us, "I am with you." When he dragged that heavy cross through the streets of Jerusalem, on his way to Calvary, he was showing us, "I am with you." When he sacrificed himself on the cross, he told us once and for all, "I am with you."

Jesus *is* with us in our suffering. You may have shared your painful stories with friends or relatives, or maybe you've sought counseling and shared it with a therapist or with a spiritual director. But God is the only one who has seen every detail of what you've been through. He knows what happened firsthand. He knows what is in your heart. He knows the pain you carry with you every day. He sees how hard you try to be faithful and do the right thing. He is with you.

One thing I've learned in all the suffering I've had over the years is that when I don't feel his presence, sometimes it's because I've drifted away from him. Sometimes he stays at a distance so that *I will go in search of him.* Yet, he's still there. He's still with me, but he's giving me the opportunity to grow in my faith by making the effort to be closer to him. He wants it to be my choice. So that's the question I pose to you if you are doubting that God cares: Could he be calling you to come closer to him?

In Romans 8:28, Saint Paul assures us that if we are faithful to God and love him, he will take our circumstances, no matter how bleak and depressing they might seem, and use them for our good. He will make something good happen out of all this.

Why does God do this? Because he needs you. Jesus is saying, "I'm with you," but he's also saying, "I need you." In the end, God wants you to heal and move forward so that you can be happy, but he also wants you to do this because *he needs you.*

You are a *survivor* of a terribly devastating event, and God needs you to help others who will be following in your footsteps, looking for answers, looking for compassion and understanding, but most of all, looking for someone to give them hope. They want to know that their time to mourn will come to an end, and that there will be a time ahead when they will be able to smile, to feel happy, and to dance again. Getting through this important time in your life, and finding the peace and healing you seek, will in turn help you to be that person for someone who will be suffering through a divorce in the future. And that is one of the greatest gifts you can give.

I hope this book has given you some sense of clarity and consolation about the annulment process. It truly is a tool at your disposal for healing and moving forward to a happier chapter of life. Count on my prayers for you as you proceed.

SPECIAL THANKS TO CONTRIBUTORS

I am so grateful to the men and women who have contributed to this book. Some have requested to remain anonymous, and others are named below. Each person who offered us a glimpse into the challenges and triumphs they faced in their own divorce and annulment experiences have my respect and gratitude for sharing their pain so that we can all learn and become better for it.

Chris Easterly

Chris Easterly is a professional screenwriter and independent filmmaker. A graduate of the Warner Brothers Television Writers Workshop, his writing credits include *Past Life* (Fox), *Unnatural History* (Cartoon Network), and *The Shunning* (Hallmark Channel). His divorce memoir, *Falling Forward*, was selected as an exclusive Amazon Kindle Single. Represented by Bauman Management in Los Angeles, he is a member of the Writers Guild of America. **email:cteast00@yahoo.com**

Dan Flaherty

Dan Flaherty is a freelance writer and author. His novel, *Fulcrum*, captures Irish Catholic life in postwar Boston and his most recent book, *Great 1980s Sports Moments*, is the definitive look at the players, games, and teams that defined his generation of sports fans. Dan lives west of Boston.
website: www.thesportsnotebook.com
email: danflaherty21070@yahoo.com

Rose Sweet

Rose Sweet is a Catholic author, speaker, and creator of the *Surviving Divorce* video program. She is passionate about divorce ministry and works with dioceses across the country assisting both petitioners and respondents in the annulment process.

website: www.rosesweet.com
email: rose@rosesweet.com